BUSINESS SMARTS™

BUSINESS FINANCE MADE EASY

MARLENE C. PITURRO

PRICE STERN SLOAN

Los Angeles

A TERN ENTERPRISES BOOK

© 1990 by Tern Enterprises, Inc.

Published by Price Stern Sloan, Inc.
360 North La Cienega Boulevard, Los Angeles, California 90048

Printed in the United States of America
9 8 7 6 5 4 3 2 1

Library of Congress Cataloging-in-Publication Data
Piturro, Marlene
    Business finance made easy / Marlene Piturro.
        p. cm. -- (Business smarts)
    ISBN 0-89586-768-0
    1. Corporations--Finance. 2. Finance. Personal. I. Title.
    II. Series.
    HG4026.P59   1990   89-24308
    658.15--dc20   CIP

Business Finance Made Easy
was prepared and produced by
Tern Enterprises, Inc.
15 West 26th Street
New York, New York 10010

Cover design: Paul Matarazzo
Cover illustration: Donald Richey
Interior design: Lynn Fischer

ACKNOWLEDGMENTS

Many people helped me to bring my view of the world of finance into focus. I'd like to thank particularly my experts—Mr. Henry Mertens and others at Bristol-Myers, Inc., Ms. Berhan Legesse at Pepsico, Inc., Mr. Sheldon Jacobs and Dr. Herbert Froehlich for their generous contributions of time and information. Dr. Harry Stevens of Ann Arbor, Michigan, and Ms. Susanna Opper of New York City deserve special thanks for their input on electronic networking technology.

Dr. Ben Wiseman and the staff of the Mercy College Library receive my gratitude for facilitating my research efforts. To my colleagues at the National Writers Union, Dick Leonard, Bob Reiser and Paul Zuckerman, thanks for your support.

To Mr. Ian Brett of the Hong Kong Economic Trade Office and Mr. Bryan Neal of Hongkong-Shanghai Bank, I owe profound thanks for all their help on my view of the globalization of finance.

This book could not have been written without the help of my right-hand person, Komal Singh, who acted as proofreader and house manager. Last, thanks to my family, Howard, Vicky, Kirk and Shivana, who made a lot of noise but managed to help see this project through to completion.

CONTENTS

Business Finance Made Easy is for everyone who reads about RUF's, NIC's, TRUF's and MUFF's and thinks he's in a comic strip, or who imagines that CAT's, TIGR's, LYON's, STAG's and ZEBRA's are things you find in the zoo.

This book will demystify the world of corporate finance and make accessible the secrets and techniques that top decision-makers have at their command. I will do this by:

• giving an overview of the key financial trends operating now

• describing rapidly changing institutions

• explaining basic business building blocks

• providing the means to understand financial statements

• showing how to use the newspapers and a personal computer to keep financially savvy

• explaining the current "merger mania" corporate acquisition activity

• pulling it all together and laying the foundation for an individual's financial future based on expert trend spotting

When you finish reading **Business Finance Made Easy**, chances are you'll be able to say, "Now I understand what the world of corporate finance is all about and how I can apply it to my own life."

Chapter 1

WHERE THE WORLD IS NOW

When I was a kid things were simple. You saved your money in a piggy bank, and when you had enough (according to the parental authorities) you went to the savings bank and deposited it using your passbook. When you got older you graduated to your very own checkbook at a commercial bank. Maybe you bought a house and got the mortgage from the same bank where you had that very first savings account. Every year you did your taxes, eventually you drew up a will, maybe purchased some life insurance. Life was fairly simple.

It has been only twenty years since my ideas about finance were laid down, but it seems like several light-years or star dates ago because things have changed so much. Deregulation of financial institutions in recent years has made it hard to tell the difference between banks and other financial institutions. The staggering array of new products and services—including credit cards, certificates of deposit and the world of acronyms (all of which will be explained later)—ATM's, CAT's, TIGR's, LYON's, STAG's, ZEBRA's, ICON's, BEC's, FRN's, RUF's, TRUF's, MUFF's, SNIF's and COLT's—is almost too much to expect anyone to master.

As consumers we have an array of choices because as the financial scene, both domestic and international, has gotten more complicated and more integrated it affects the financial products we buy and the way they are delivered. Let's look at the major trends that have changed our financial lives.

The Deregulation of Finance

Since the 1970s the financial industry has seen a loosening of federal and state regulations that have helped financial institutions to innovate, introduce new methods and instruments and to enter new areas of business. Many factors have been responsible for the trend toward deregulation, including advances in computer technology, growth in income and the diversification of financial products. The election of Ronald Reagan as President in 1980 spearheaded a "hands-off" policy toward financial institutions, particularly with regard to corporate mergers and acquisitions. Although the democratically controlled Congress has continually fought for increasing regulation, particularly for the troubled savings-and-loan institutions and the "junk bond" industry, President George Bush seems likely to follow the "hands off" policies of his predecessor and mentor—unless he is forced to intervene by an economic downturn precipitated by rising inflation or a spate of bank failures.

While there have been many different forms of deregulation, the major changes have been as follows:

• the lifting of restrictions on interest rates charged by banks and other institutions and investment services

• the removal of barriers to the entry of foreign financial institutions to the United States

• the demise of constraints on the types of activities in which financial institutions are allowed to engage

The removal of restrictions on interest rates and on funding limits of certain instruments is almost complete in all of the major industrialized countries. There are still a few exceptions, mainly in Japan.

The types of activities that financial institutions can engage in is what enables you as a consumer to pick from such a wide variety of choices. There are still some important exceptions, particularly in the United States: investment banking and deposit banking must be kept separate (although, experts say, this will probably change in the next several years), monitoring of exchange controls, and specification of what a particular financial institution is allowed to do. Even the Glass-Steagall Act, which prohibits interstate banking, is due to fall in 1990. These regulations and control systems were enacted at a time, mostly in the 1930s through 1950s, to help small banks stay alive and able to compete against giant banking monopolies that would gain increasing power if left to grow unchecked. Deposit banking, as opposed to investment or commercial banking, existed as a separate system for more than fifty years to protect the homeowner's equity-building vehicle, home ownership and the mortgage that make it possible.

As the barriers continue to tumble, there will be an even wider array of products and services provided by commercial banks, savings banks, stockbrokers and securities houses. Shopping around for the best interest rates, minimum lending limits, liquidity, maturity rates and resale value in the secondary market (how much the investor can resell the financial instrument for before its maturity date) is becoming ever more attractive. Someday soon we may see the establishment in this country of the kinds of banks that have existed for many years in Switzerland, Germany and Austria, the so-called "universal banks" where financial institutions are allowed to transact any kind of financial business that the market will bear.

The Internationalization of Finance

The deregulation of financial industries, particularly in the United States, Japan, the United Kingdom, France and Italy, has led to a greater willingness to do business globally.

Computer-aided transaction processing now makes it possible to carry out business twenty-four hours a day. That's why companies with a strong domestic presence can now reach out to the whole world.

Take the example of Hong Kong based Hongkong-Shanghai Bank. This venerable institution, 125 years old in 1990, has built a dazzling global presence in the past twenty years. It's now a five-legged creature, made up of the following components:

- commercial banking
- stockbroking and merchant banking (banking devoted to the needs of the middle market—$5 million to $100 million—of commercial enterprises)
- insurance
- investment holding
- finance

Some information about its holdings may surprise you. For example, did you know that Marine Midland Bank is now 100 percent owned by Hongkong Bank? The bank's own figures show an impressive list of holdings:

- British Bank of the Middle East (100 percent)
- Hongkong Bank of Canada (100 percent)
- Hang Seng Bank (61.5 percent)
- Hongkong Bank of Australia (100 percent)
- Cathay Pacific Airlines (16.4 percent)
- Wardley Holdings Co. (100 percent)

We don't feel the presence of Hongkong Bank on our Marine Midland system in the United States because the parent company takes a hands-off approach. As long as Marine Midland meets its strategic goals, it's free to transact business any way it pleases. Later in the book we'll contrast this with the more hands-on approach that Americans take when they acquire a company.

Put it together and what have you got? A globe-spanning operation that runs from Asia to America to Europe—the largest bank in the world, with the capability through any of its five legs to execute virtually any economic transaction imaginable and desirable. It has the most sophisticated transaction processing computer equipment in the world, capable of processing 100,000 transactions every hour. Its fabled inner reserves are reported to be nearly $3 billion. (If you have a hard time conceptualizing what $3 billion means in real terms, $3 billion represents the combined 1988 revenues of these top U.S. companies: Avon Products Inc., Gulf & Western Inc. and Ingersoll Rand. Most American banks keep only a tiny fraction of their revenues as reserves—perhaps 5 to 10 percent.)

Is there a banker anywhere in the world who wouldn't give his or her eyeteeth for access to the 1 billion consumers in China, who have had practically no exposure to broad-scale commercial banking? Even despite recent turmoil, China is opening itself up to commercial banking as part of its overall economic reform. As the eight special enterprise zones in China have boomed in the last five years, giving Chinese and foreign entrepreneurs a taste of capitalism, Hongkong Bank is right there, poised to be China's de facto central bank and to thoroughly modernize a rather archaic system. Hongkong Bank, both by itself and with its Chinese-owned subsidiary, Hang Seng Bank, has the best chance to penetrate that huge market. If any bank can resolve the ambiguity of operating as both a global capitalist bank and a sovereign communist bank, it's Hongkong Bank.

The goal of an international banker might go something like this when he or she talks about a global bank: "I'd like my customer to be able to buy renminbi from a regional office in Zaire, swap yen for baht to finance an acquisition in Portugal and enlist my bank to manage an Egyptian investment portfolio." Such flexibility is facilitated by several factors on the international scene:

• twenty-four-hour data processing has spurred growth in the number of foreign financial institutions in both the primary centers (New York, London and Tokyo), and the secondary financial centers (Hong Kong, Singapore, Paris and Frankfurt)

- dramatically increased holdings of real assets (buildings, and financial institutions owned directly and indirectly by overseas businesspeople)

- a marked increase in the flow of funds across national boundaries

Here are some examples of what the "internationalization of finance" means in real terms: The Bank of England estimated in July 1988 that trading in foreign currencies had doubled in two years, from $200 billion to $400 billion. The increase since 1975 has been estimated at at least 20 percent, if not more. Meanwhile, holdings in foreign assets, particularly by Japan, have increased just as dramatically: In 1981 Japan had $32 billion invested in its portfolio; by 1986 it owned $258 billion in foreign assets. Even greater momentum is expected as Europe moves toward unification in 1992, when, among other things, its program for dismantling the remaining obstacles to movements in capital will be in place.

The American financial community is watching warily as Europe moves toward a completely integrated economic community of its twelve member countries. While trade barriers will fall between them, making it much easier to do business between members than it is now, many outsiders, the United States included, fear a fortress mentality that may make U.S.-Europe trade more difficult to accomplish than it is at present.

New, Improved Instruments

The choice of investments is so broad right now that it can be very confusing for an individual to select something that is right for him or her. What's important to see, though, is how the offerings of new financial instruments tie in with the globalization of banking.

Financial innovation is both the cause and effect of internationalization. Different products arising in different financial markets around the world have stimulated demand. This has made countries interdependent as never before. These new instruments have been created in response to new demand, arising from factors such as the volatility of exchange and interest rates and increased demands for capital requirements to fund the many new and growing commercial ventures in many countries. The entrepreneurial spirit seems to be thriving around the globe.

As the lines drawn between the various types of financial institutions continue to fade, we see all kinds of transactions offered by commercial banks, savings and loans, insurance companies, real estate developers and investment banks. The kinds of transactions are so sophisticated—*e.g.,* asset swaps, currency options trading, interest-rate swaps, interest-rate futures and precious metals trading, just to name a few—that understanding them seems mind-boggling. Later in this book we'll look at the instruments most appropriate for the average, "garden variety" investor—anyone interested in his or her financial well-being, individuals who follow the financial news in *The New York Times* and *The Wall Street Journal*, investors who use insurance brokers or perhaps stockbrokers to help make sense of their family's particular financial goals and needs.

Behind all this innovation is a fancy new word: **securitization**. Securitization means that you have to use an asset that you currently own as collateral. Securitization makes the innovators feel secure, knowing that something is behind the product should something go wrong. Assets that companies can now offer as collateral may surprise you: Car loans, credit card receivables, recreational-vehicle loans and equipment loans are being used to create new types of securities, thus providing liquidity for the underwriter. Most of the innovation has occurred in the unregulated international markets, although Americans have followed suit cautiously.

Internationally, the process of securitization has acted as the glue for the world financial market by widening the entry of nonfinancial and financial companies to raise short-, medium- and long-term funds in any currency and convert them into other currencies, while shielding themselves from exposure to risk.

What Does This All Mean to You?

Deregulation, internationalization and innovation backed by securitization all make for an interesting and complex financial system. As world output increases and less-developed countries industrialize, the developed countries will become even more service-oriented. As products diversify because of so much increased participation by both new and old market players, the cost and flexibility of financial instruments will increase.

Further improvements in telecommunications and transaction processing will make the mix even more interesting because costs will be lowered and access made easier for home-based investors. Savings institutions and deposit-taking institutions will be investing their assets over a larger area in order to diversify their holdings and also to improve their rate of return.

The individual investor will have to learn to be more flexible and responsible to keep up with all this. It just won't do to stash your money in a low-yield savings passbook anymore; you'll have to follow yields and even switch some money to certificates of deposit or money-market funds, depending on the relative interest rates.

Let's not forget one more very important item—with all this complexity and diversity in financial institutions, there's an ever-growing need for competent, intelligent people to learn it all and administer it properly. Opportunities have never been greater for a career in finance, and that includes professional opportunities both in U.S. and international banking.

So, whether you're an individual investor, someone thinking about a career in finance or you just want to keep up with the conversation when people start talking about their financial "instruments," let's forge ahead.

Chapter **2**

Do any of us really save the way we should? Government statistics show that Americans save at a rate of 4 percent annually, while our Asian counterparts, particularly the Japanese, sock money away at rates three or four times greater than we do. Discipline isn't easy, and everyone I know (myself included) uses his or her plastic money entirely too much. However, there are a number of ways, most of them painless, to put money away for emergencies, unemployment dry spells, dream purchases and retirement. The two easiest ways are:

- Day-to-day savings

Commercial and savings banks offer various plans with flexibility and convenience. You park spare cash there that earns compound interest daily, and make withdrawals and deposits as necessary. As you comparison-shop, look for higher interest rates on savings and checking, low minimum balances, free checking, incentives, funds transfer to other accounts and the convenience of one statement for checking and savings.

- Vacation clubs

This is the easiest way to force yourself to put money away, in amounts from $2 to $50 a week, for that once-a-year splurge. The interest rate is nominal, around 5 percent, but it's a pleasant way to enforce self-discipline.

Getting Serious

Once you're hooked on the idea of casual savings, you're ready to move up a few notches to slightly more sophisticated instruments:

- Money-market accounts

These are a cross between savings and checking and carry interest rates 1 or 2 percent higher than most savings accounts. Minimum investments vary, but $2,500 is common. Money-market accounts make sense for individuals, small businesses and even nonprofit organizations who want competitive rates, unlimited access to funds and FDIC insurance. Usually, you can arrange for money market funds to be transferred to your checking account or another kind of fund on a day's notice. All this presupposes that you are savvy about changes in interest rates. If you're not, read on.

- Fixed-rate savings-investor certificates (Certificates of Deposit, or CD's)

You've really got your toe in the financial waters now. Your immediate demands for liquidity, or available cash, are satisfied by your day-to-day savings and money-market accounts, and you're ready to get serious. CD's are for longer-range savings goals, but there's a slight catch—you aren't allowed to touch your money for the term of the certificate without being assessed a penalty for early withdrawal. But don't let this stipulation make you nervous—CD's are available in terms from three months to eight years, and for a minimum of $1,000, which gives you a good degree of flexibility in determining just how long you think you can do "without" the money. You get a guaranteed money-market rate for the life of the CD, but you have to feel comfortable before "locking in" to a rate. In an inflationary period with interest rates escalating, you'd want to pick a shorter term CD. Many long-term CD's give you a monthly interest check or credit your interest payments automatically to your checking account.

Later

Want to start putting aside some money for retirement? There are two common types of plans:

- Individual Retirement Accounts (IRA's)

The Tax Reform Act of 1986 pretty much spoiled this vehicle for most people. Previously, individuals were allowed to make a tax-free IRA contribution of up to $2,000 each year; taxes would be paid when you withdrew the money, after you retired. But Congress decided that was too much of a good thing and in 1986 stopped people with company-sponsored retirement plans from deducting their IRA contributions. High earners—$50,000 for a couple, and $35,000 for a single taxpayer—can't deduct their IRA payments anymore, although tax-free savings for those of lesser means are still possible. IRA's are still a good vehicle for investing up to $2,000 in a retirement plan for people who don't participate in a company-sponsored plan. People on salary might inquire about a 401-K (corporate) or 503-C (nonprofit) plan for tax-deferred savings.

- Keogh plan

This is a special retirement plan for people with self-employment income. Even if you have a company-sponsored plan at your "real" job, if you earn extra money as an independent contractor or in your own small business you can have a Keogh for your own business. If you qualify for a

Keogh plan you may deposit either 25 percent of your self-employed income, or up to $30,000 a year, whichever is less, and exclude that total amount, plus all the interest you earn, from your federal income taxes.

Theoretically, you can have an IRA and a Keogh plan at the same time, but only if you have separate sources of income for each. IRA's are generally funded through earnings from a salaried position, while Keoghs are for the self-employed. So if you have a small business on the side, in addition to your regular job, you might be contributing to both plans, especially if you wanted or needed to sock away a lot of money for retirement.

Municipal Securities

For investors who want safety and don't like to pay taxes on interest, municipal securities are just the thing. "Munis" are the debt obligations of states, their political subdivisions and certain agencies. Nearly 38,000 state and local governments can issue such securities to raise money for public purposes such as water and sewer systems, schools, housing, highways and hospitals. The interest income from munis is exempt from federal income taxes and, in most states, exempt from state tax for securities issued within that state. Interest rates on municipal bonds vary widely and depend, generally, on the term (length of time until the muni matures) and riskiness of the municipality issuing the bond. Rates are generally in the 6.5 to 10 percent range. The tax-exempt feature permits state and local governments to borrow at lower interest rates than corporations to accomplish their goals. Many think that investing in munis is only for the rich, since the minimum investment is usually $5,000. However, certain funds and trusts start with investments of $1,000.

When it comes to safety, munis have an extraordinary track record when compared, say, to the stock market. To determine the relative quality of munis, many investors rely on the ratings provided by the two major rating agencies, Moody's Investors Service, Inc., and Standard & Poor's Corporation. Here are the two scales of classifications, with "triple A" being the best, or "prime," indicating the lowest credit risk:

CREDIT RISK	MOODY'S	S&P
Prime	Aaa	AAA
Excellent	Aa	AA
Upper medium	A-1, A	A
Lower medium	Baa-1, Baa	BBB
Speculative	BA	BB
Very speculative	B, Caa	B, CCC
Default	Ca, C	D

Note: A + or – attached to an S&P rating indicates that a credit is considered to be in the upper or lower segment of the rating category.

TYPES OF MUNIS

Most munis are sold in serial form—that is, a portion of the issue comes due periodically, anywhere from six months to fifty years. Thus, a large municipal-bond issue will usually consist of many separate serial maturities, often each with its own coupon rate. So a municipality may decide to break the financing of a very large project—for example, a new college campus—into small pieces, raising money for the project as it goes along. Let's say the new building will cost $50 million and the entire project will be completed in twenty years. The issuer may sell $25 million worth of bonds immediately, and the balance in smaller batches as the project progresses. New-comers to the muni market can feel a bit frustrated when they want to get going purchasing munis and there's nothing suit-able "out there" to buy. You just have to wait until the right issue comes along (there are muni-bond salespeople who can keep you informed of new issues) and then plunk down the money.

Most bonds will be in denominations of $5,000. Notes are usually sold with a minimum of $25,000. There are many types of bonds and notes. Some of the most common are:

- General obligation bonds

Payment of interest on, and principal of, general obligation bonds is secured by the full faith and credit of the issuer, and usually supported by either the issuer's unlimited or limited taxing power. "Full faith and credit of the issuer" means that in the almost unthinkable event of a default by the issuer, the bond holders would be among the first in line of many creditors waiting to get paid when the issuer gets back on its feet. The "unthinkable" almost happened in 1975 to New York City bond holders. As the city hovered on the brink of default, bond holders held their breath—but New York was rescued by the Municipal Assistance Corporation (MAC), a special agency created to bring the city back to financial health. If New York City had defaulted, bond holders, along with city employees waiting for paychecks and suppliers waiting for payment for goods and services, would have had to wait and see if the state and federal regulators would have stepped in to help.

- Special tax bonds

Interest and principal on these bonds are secured by a specified tax or series of taxes, such as a gas tax or utility franchise tax. If the bond also carries the issuer's pledge of full faith, credit and taxing power, it is classified as a general obligation bond.

- Revenue bonds

Revenue bonds are secured by a pledge of net or gross income derived from tolls, charges or rents paid by users of the facility built with the proceeds of the bond issue. Highways, bridges, airports, water- and sewage-treatment facilities are examples of public projects financed by revenue bonds.

OTHER ISSUERS OF BONDS AND NOTES

In addition to municipalities, there are other types of entities that issue bonds and notes. The concept remains the same: The issuer, whether it is a public utility, public-housing authority or urban-renewal project, uses the promise of future revenue to sell bonds to the public.

Unlike many other financial instruments, which have to be traded by specially trained and licensed people and are virtually incomprehensible, municipal securities are purchased mainly by individual investors. While stocks, swaps and other more glamorous trades require the intervention of a third party, individuals can and do buy munis on their own initiative.

OTHER OPTIONS

If you're not the type to put all your eggs in one basket, then a portfolio of munis may be right for you. Additionally, for investors who find the $5,000 minimum investment in an individual bond too steep, there are other options:

- Unit-trust investment

This is a tax-exempt portfolio of municipal bonds with a minimum investment of $1,000. With a unit-trust investment, individuals can purchase units of a trust, acquiring shared interest in a diversified bond portfolio offering a balance of yield, size and security that they might not be able to afford individually. Bond brokers buy and sell these trusts, and the commission is modest, roughly 4 percent.

- Municipal-bond funds

Again, these combine individual issues into a portfolio available to the individual investor. Yields are usually competitive, about 2 to 4 percent above money-market rates, and you can usually switch from a money market into these, and vice versa, fairly easily.

Very Safe . . .

If you *really* want to play it safe, there's the old reliable Treasury bill (T-bill). These are U.S. government issues having an original maturity of one year or less. They are available with a minimum face value of $10,000, and in $5,000 increments thereafter. T-bills are an excellent investment because of the high liquidity, variety of maturities and lack of credit risk. The downside? You pay federal taxes on the interest.

And Now, for Jungle Stalkers

Now we get to the part about CAT's (Certificates of Accrual on Treasury Securities), TIGR's (Treasury Income Growth Receipts), LYON's (Liquid Yield Option Zeros Notes), STAG's (Sterling Transferable Accruing Government Securities) and ZEBRA's (Zero-Coupon Eurosterling Bearer of Registered Securities). At least we know that the financial mavens who first thought up these products had a good sense of humor.

These securities were designed to appeal to the more adventurous sort of investor. The "jungle variety" CAT's, TIGR's and the like are known generically as zero-coupon bonds. They are municipal bonds for which the interest has been "stripped away" to zero at what would usually be your time to receive a dividend, and reinvested, to be paid out only on full maturity. You don't receive periodic dividends, but you get it all back in the end. Thus, their initial purchase price is low. They have been deeply discounted. For example, an investment of $5,000 will return to you approximately $15,000 in fifteen years. Unfortunately, you have to forgo interest payments that you would ordinarily receive with other bonds. As we mentioned, the interest is plowed back into the bond; that's why you can buy them so cheaply. When the bond comes to full maturity you pay no tax on either principle or interest, so if you're thinking of using zero-coupon bonds for college or retirement planning, you get all that money tax free.

You have to be a pretty sharp investor to spot just the right time to buy zero-coupon bonds. First of all, they aren't available all the time—only when a municipality decides to issue a zero-coupon instrument as opposed to the more usual muni bond, which pays a periodic dividend. You also want to be careful that you buy a muni zero-coupon bond if you want all the interest to be tax-free. This is particularly important if you're using zero coupons to finance your child's education. If you buy taxable zero coupons, the recipient, your child, will have to pay the taxes on the interest, thereby eroding the money left for college.

There are corporate zero-coupon bonds available, but they are taxable because corporate earnings are taxable. Generally, these are fairly speculative and have a higher yield than the muni zero coupons.

Because zero coupons are a specialized form of investment, you might want to consult a bond broker to let you know when issues meeting your needs come across his or her path.

The Future

Financial innovation is rapidly changing the face of investing. Institutions that handle investors' money are constantly thinking of new ways to offer products to jaded and wary buyers. Today it's unbundled stock units. Tomorrow, who knows what? The best strategy is to stick with the basics for your emergency, college and retirement needs and dabble in the more exciting new ventures if you feel comfortable that the basics have been secured. Just keep in mind that our ever more complex international financial community means more choices are available than ever before.

Chapter 3

HOW TO READ THE FINANCIAL NEWS

You're driving home after work and turn on the radio to hear the business news. "The stock market is up today," says the announcer. Or you pick up the business section of *The New York Times* and the markets-and-investing section of *The Wall Street Journal*. You buy books and magazines with year-end summaries or news of fast-breaking trends. You may even get your business news on-line via the rapidly growing number of electronic bulletin boards.

All of the ways we get our business news are based on one common underlying assumption—that studying the past provides a way to predict the future. "Where's the market heading?" is what every investor wants to know. You're looking at the present and the past, but the only thing that matters is the future.

Most professionals who market-watch for a living use a variety of techniques, ranging from the almost mystical to strict reliance on formulas.

What are some of the things that even the novice investor can use to spot trends? Can this be done without a great deal of expertise? The answer is a qualified "yes." You can get some feeling of where the economy is headed by analyzing the following:

• Are big-ticket items like cars and houses selling? If so, consumers have confidence in the economy, that it's on an upward trend.

• How are interest rates going? If short-term rates are up on money-market funds and T-bills, that means investors are scared of the stock market, or perhaps the economy in general. They're putting their money and faith into short-term, nonspeculative places, usually with a wait-and-see attitude about which direction the stock market will turn. Rising long-term rates may indicate problems with inflation. As the cost of borrowing money becomes higher, everything else costs more in a continuously upward spiral.

• Are bond prices falling and yields rising? This may be a sign of an inflationary trend and a poor indication for the stock market because investors are all clamoring to get into a safe investment and avoid the more perilous up-and-down movements of the market.

• Is the Federal Reserve raising the prime rate (the interest rate at which banks lend money out to their best institutional customers)? That could mean it wants to slow down an overheated economy, because as it costs more to borrow money, people will slow down on their borrowing.

• Are oil, precious-metals and commodity prices fluctuating? What, if any, world events does this involve?

• Is the Dow Jones average up but the Standard & Poors average fairly steady? That could mean investor confidence only in blue chip stocks, but not in the market overall.

Market Forecasting: Another Way of Saying Tricky Business

It's terribly tempting to say that market pundits are always wrong. The market zigs when experts say it's going to zag. But the truth is that they're trying to predict the market's future behavior based on an exceedingly complex set of factors, some economic, some political and some psychological. The investors who follow their advice, or try to come up with formulas of their own, buy stock when they expect prices to advance and sell when they think prices will decline.

Read All About It!

Your daily journey through *The New York Times* and *The Wall Street Journal* should put you on solid ground in keeping up with the financial news. However, if you're looking for other slants, there is a slew of periodicals you can try. All are available on newsstands.

Barron's

The Financial Times

Money

Financial World

Sylvia Porter's Personal Finance

Investor's Daily

The Journal of Commerce

BusinessWeek

Forbes

Fortune

Inc.

Entrepreneur

Venture

Is market forecasting sensible? Lord John Maynard Keynes, probably the twentieth century's most famous economist, summarized the state-of-the-art some years ago:

"Professional investment may be likened to those newspaper competitions in which the competitors have to pick out the six prettiest faces from a hundred photographs, the prize being awarded to the competitor whose choice most nearly corresponds to the average preferences of the competitors as a whole; so each competitor has to pick, not those faces which he himself finds prettiest, but those which he thinks likeliest to catch the fancy of the other competitors, all of whom are looking at the problem from the same point of view. It is not a case of choosing those which, to the best of one's judgment, are really the prettiest, nor even those which average opinion genuinely thinks the prettiest. We have reached the third degree where we devote our intelligences to anticipating what average opinion expects the average opinion to be."

Daily Digging—Newspapers

With the understanding that you may do just as well by gazing into your crystal ball as by relying on expert opinion, we're now going to assume that predicting the stock market is something that every intelligent investor can and should do. Sheldon Jacobs, writer, researcher, publisher and an investor who turned his avocation—dabbling in investments as a way to generate extra income—into a vocation, now tells us how he reads the daily newspapers to keep abreast of market trends. Incidentally, Jacobs did so well at his avocation that he quit his job in the NBC-TV research department to concentrate on writing books and newsletters about investing.

THE NEW YORK TIMES

To get an overview of the news, scan the first three lead articles, the editorial page, the "Op Ed" page and the "Letters to the Editor." Why not turn right away to the "Business" section? Says Jacobs: "You want to start every business day with a feeling about what important events are happening in the world. The stock market so often reacts to perceived rather than actual changes in the world that you have to understand what might make investors jittery." He emphasizes the importance of reading the "Op Ed" page and "Letters to the Editor." "Most reporters are not experts, and don't express all the important opinions on the subject. The letter-writer, on the other hand, is an expert in his subject, and what he says is very revealing."

Once you're finished with the overview of the paper, you should turn to "Business Day" (section D). Scan the front page for the three or four major business stories of the day. Are they about interest rates? Technology? Plant closings? Legal issues? International trade? Get an overall impression of the major news. The market is more responsive to news than it used to be because of the growing proportion of stock-trading volume accounted for by institutions, the increasing emphasis on profits over dividends and the increasing activities of governmental agencies such as the SEC and prosecutors' use of the Racketeer Influenced and Corrupt Organizations Act (RICO) in cases of business and corporate abuses.

You might think that institutions would be more interested in long-term strategies than in short-term factors. However, the herd mentality dominates in institutional trading. One industry leader, rightly or wrongly sensing a change in important economic trends, might trigger an institutional stampede. This is what happened, at least partially, on Black Monday, October 19, 1987. While there was no precipitating world or even economic catastrophe to trigger the 500-point plunge on the New York Stock Exchange, a number of computer programs, all measuring the same economic indicators, went "beep" simultaneously, triggering massive institutional dumping of stocks and widespread panic. Post-Black Monday governmental and industry panels studying the phenomenon of programmed trading rightly pointed out the disastrous impact of computers all programmed to say "sell" without taking all relevant information into account. Programmed trading has been severely curtailed as a result of Black Monday, returning just a bit of control to human stock analysts.

Next, review the "Business Digest" in the upper left corner (see below). The four major indicators are:

• Dow

The Dow Jones Industrial (DJI) average of thirty blue-chip stocks (prominent companies with long and successful histories) is the oldest and most respected barometer of the stock market. Why are there only thirty stocks in the DJI calculation? And why those particular stocks? The DJI's purpose is to spot trends, not give an in-depth view of how the market is doing. We look at the Dow and its thirty selected stocks with a long and very detailed history on a daily, monthly, quarterly and even yearly basis as our basic indicator of market strength.

• Dollar

This is a comparison of the U.S. dollar to the Japanese yen. An upward trend in the yen indicates a decline in the value of the dollar, and vice versa.

• Gold

The Comex (commodities exchange) Spot gives a snapshot of how gold was traded worldwide during the past twenty-four hours. A figure of "-$3.00" indicates that the price per ounce dropped by three dollars. Many investors are very interested in the prices of gold and other "precious metals" such as

D<small>BUSINESS</small>igest

FRIDAY, SEPTEMBER 8, 1989

DOW	DOLLAR	GOLD	BONDS
30 Industrials	vs. Japanese Yen	Comex Spot	30-Year Treasuries
2,706.88	146.65 Yen	$360.20	8.11%
-12.91	+0.55 Yen	-$1.40	+0.01%

silver and platinum. As a matter of fact, some investors avoid stocks, money-market funds, bonds and other investments in favor of gold and other metals. You can buy precious metals in several forms—as coins, as bullion (bars of various weights), as stocks or as futures (meaning you'll pay a certain price at a specified date sometime in the future). Gold represents the ultimate in financial security and allure to a certain segment of the investing community.

• Bonds

This column gives the interest yield on Treasury bills with a maturity date of thirty years. Generally, high interest rates indicate that investors are nervous about putting their money in stocks, so they're investing in bonds. You have to study this column over time to get a good feel for directionality.

Next, turn to the second page of "Business Day," D2. In the upper left corner is a commentary or news story on an interesting trend or development. Get a feel for the person being quoted. If the person seems glib or superficial, take his advice with a grain of salt. If, however, you sense that that person knows what he or she is talking about, follow the advice if it's in line with your investment goals. Also on that page, in the lower right quadrant, is an index of all companies in that day's paper (see opposite). That's the place to look if you're following developments in a particular company.

Perhaps the heart of the business section lies in the "Market Indicators" column (see page 28), a summary of consolidated trading. Let's take a close look at it. "The Dow: Minute by Minute" tells you a lot more than the common statement about the market, "The Dow closed up." It indicates the market's peaks and valleys over the 10:00 A.M.-to-4:00 P.M. trading period. You'll want to be aware of sudden shifts in trading, which could be triggered by any number of factors, including a major world event such as the assassination of a country's leader, an important announcement such as a corporate acquisition or merger or the unveiling of an exciting new product by a major company.

Also notice the "S&P Components" graph, which tells you how industrials, transportation, utilities and financial stocks fared on the previous days. The NASDAQ (National Association of Security Dealers of Automated Quotations) Issues and AMEX (American Stock Exchange) Issues are other exchanges, distinct from the New York Stock Exchange, that you might want to follow. The American Stock Exchange is quite similar to the New York Stock Exchange but follows a different set of stocks. The NASDAQ is a compilation of changes in OTC (over-the-counter) market activity, based on an automated (computerized) information system.

By studying all these indicators, you're getting an overview of the entire market, how large and small companies are doing. Our market expert, Sheldon Jacobs, cautions against trying to follow individual stocks: "This is probably a waste of time for most people because you're reading yesterday's news. Leave it to the pros to clue you in to investment strategy."

COMPANY INDEX

Page numbers refer to the beginnings of articles. A dagger (†) denotes a parent company not directly mentioned in an article about a subsidiary.
"ER" in the page column refers to an entry in the Company Earnings report, which today begins on page D6.

Market Indicators

CONSOLIDATED TRADING / THURSDAY, SEPTEMBER 7, 1989

New York Stock Exchange Issues

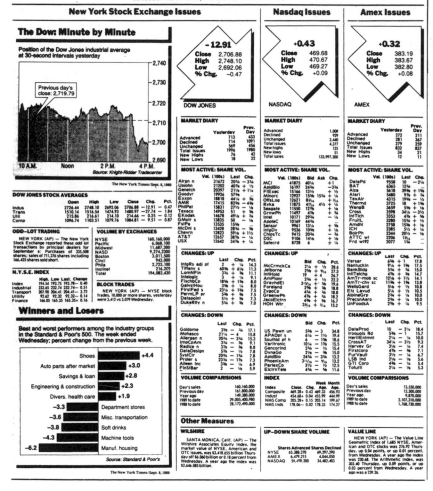

The Dow: Minute by Minute

Position of the Dow Jones industrial average at 30-second intervals yesterday

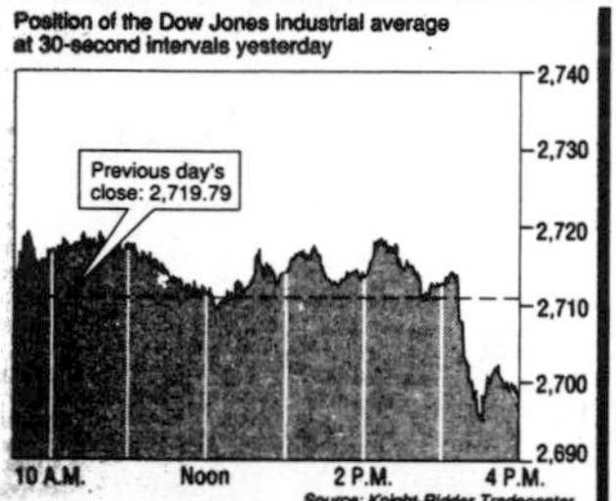

2,740
2,730
2,720
2,710
2,700
2,690
Previous day's close: 2,719.79
10 A.M.
Noon
2 P.M.
4 P.M.

Source: Knight-Ridder Tradecenter

The New York Times/Sept. 8, 1989

-12.91
Close 2,706.88
High 2,748.10
Low 2,692.06
% Chg. -0.47

DOW JONES

MARKET DIARY

	Yesterday	Prev. Day
Advanced	713	433
Declined	714	1091
Unchanged	569	456
Total Issues	1996	1980
New Highs	76	42
New Lows	18	22

MOST ACTIVE: SHARE VOL.

	Vol. (100s)	Last	Chg.
Airgn n	31672	20¾	−3¾
Upjohn	21202	40⅞	+ ½
Genetch	20397	21⅛	+1¼
Goodyr	19926	57⅜	...
Exxon	18818	44¼	+ ⅜
AMR	17415	82⅜	−4⅜
PhilPet	15831	27½	− ⅛
Texaco	14953	51	+ ⅜
EKodak	14678	49⅛	+ ¾
GMotr s	13835	50	− ⅛
FstPa	13535	15⅜	...
McDnl s	13428	28¾	− ⅜
Chevrn	12823	59⅛	+1½
AT&T	12657	38⅞	− ¼
USX	12642	34⅞	+ ¼

CHANGES: UP

	Last	Chg.	Pct.
IntgRs adj pf	2	+ ¼	14.3
Tiffany s	60⅜	+ 6⅛	11.3
LomNFin	3¾	+ ⅜	11.1
Intelogic	3	+ ¼	9.1
FischbCp	18⅜	+ 1⅜	8.0
GalvstHou	3⅜	+ ¼	8.0
FirstFed s	23¼	+ 1⅝	7.5
PermLP pr	5⅜	+ ⅜	7.5
Datapoint	5½	+ ⅜	7.3
DukeRlty n	5¾	+ ⅜	7.0

CHANGES: DOWN

	Last	Chg.	Pct.
Goldome	3⅝	− ¾	17.1
Mohasco	21¼	− 4	15.8
Allergan n	20¾	− 3¾	15.3
ImpCpAm	3¾	− ⅜	9.1
Radice n	3⅞	− ⅜	8.8
DataDesign	5⅞	− ½	7.8
SystCtr	20¾	− 1¾	7.8
Proler s	23¾	− 1⅞	7.3
Aileen Inc	3⅜	− ¼	6.9
FinStBar	2	− ⅛	5.9

VOLUME COMPARISIONS

Day's sales	160,160,000
Previous day	161,800,000
Year ago	149,380,000
1989 to date	29,005,400,980
1988 to date	28,172,490,000

DOW JONES STOCK AVERAGES

	Open	High	Low	Close	Chg.	Pct.
Indus	2726.44	2748.10	2692.06	2706.88	−12.91	− 0.47
Trans	1510.14	1516.54	1474.93	1480.97	−27.74	− 1.84
Util	215.86	216.61	214.10	214.66	− 0.25	− 0.12
Comp	1096.74	1103.51	1079.76	1084.81	− 9.51	− 0.87

ODD-LOT TRADING

NEW YORK (AP) — The New York Stock Exchange reported these odd lot transactions by principal dealers for September 6: Purchases of 335,508 shares; sales of 711,376 shares including 166,435 shares sold short.

N.Y.S.E. INDEX

	High.	Low	Last.	Change
Index	194.54	193.75	193.78	− 0.40
Industrial	233.65	232.74	232.74	− 0.51
Transport	207.90	204.41	204.41	− 3.72
Utility	92.62	92.32	92.32	− 0.14
Finance	166.05	165.35	165.35	+ 0.16

VOLUME BY EXCHANGES

NYSE	160,160,000
Pacific	6,068,100
Midwest	11,687,300
NASD	9,274,2300
Boston	3,011,500
Cinci	943,000
Phila	2,723,100
Instinet	216,200
Total	194,083,430

BLOCK TRADES

NEW YORK (AP) — NYSE block trades, 10,000 or more shares, yesterday were 3,412 vs 3,079 Wednesday.

Winners and Losers

Best and worst performers among the industry groups in the Standard & Poor's 500. The week ended Wednesday; percent change from the previous week.

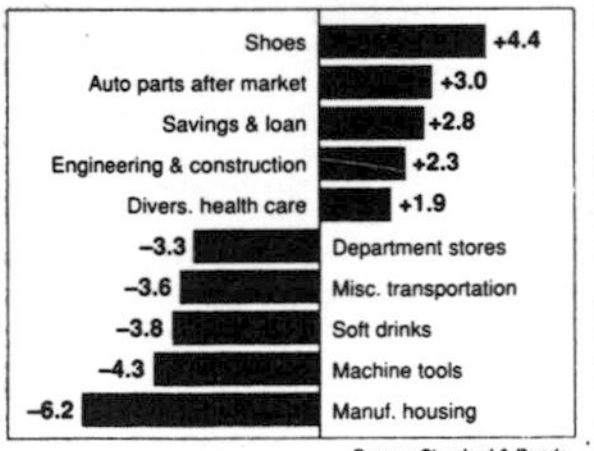

Shoes +4.4
Auto parts after market +3.0
Savings & loan +2.8
Engineering & construction +2.3
Divers. health care +1.9
-3.3 Department stores
-3.6 Misc. transportation
-3.8 Soft drinks
-4.3 Machine tools
-6.2 Manuf. housing

Source: Standard & Poor's

The New York Times/Sept. 8, 1989

Nasdaq Issues

+0.43
Close 469.68
High 470.67
Low 469.27
% Chg. +0.09

NASDAQ

MARKET DIARY

Advanced	1,008
Declined	929
Unchanged	2,440
Total issues	4,377
New highs	125
New lows	51
Total sales	133,997,300

MOST ACTIVE: SHARE VOL.

	Vol. (100s)	Bid	Ask	Chg.
MCI	41875	40¼		+1
ApldBio	16197	24¾		−3¾
FtExec	15166	13½		+ ½
Minorc	12927	15⅝	15¾	+ ¼
OffsLog	12621	8 5/16		+ 1/16
Ryka	11875	4 7/16	4½	+ ¼
Seagate	11550	12⅞		+ ⅛
GrnwPh	11497	4⅞		+ ¾
Intel	10171	29¾		− ¼
AppleC	10169	44¾		...
Sensor	9961	13¼		+ ⅜
IntgDv	9536	10⅜		+ ⅛
ChipsTc	9415	20¾		− ¾
DSC	9106	14⅛		+ ⅛
Safecrd	8728	6		+ ¼

CHANGES: UP

	Bid	Chg.	Pct.
McCrmckCa	2¼	+ ½	28.6
Jetborne	2⅝	+ 9/16	27.3
IntlHold	19	+ 4	26.7
AmPionr	2¾	+ ½	22.2
GrayhdEl	3 13/16	+ ⅝	19.6
Foreland	2⅜	+ ⅜	18.8
ZygoCp	4¾	+ ¾	18.8
GreenwPh	4⅞	+ ¾	18.2
JacoElctrn	4⅜	+ ⅝	16.7
HOH Wtr	3 5/16	+ 7/16	15.2

CHANGES: DOWN

	Bid	Chg.	Pct.
US Pawn un	5⅝	− 3	34.8
APAOpt s	6¼	− 1½	19.4
Southld pf h	6	− 1⅜	18.6
Varitronic	10¼	− 1⅞	15.5
GencorInd	2¾	− ½	15.4
DynaGp	2⅛	− ⅜	15.0
ApldBio	24¾	− 3¾	13.2
PhoenixAm	3 11/16	− 9/16	13.2
ParlexCp	3½	− ½	12.5
ElctrnTele	4¾	− ⅝	11.6

INDEX

Index	Close.	Chg.	Week Ago.	Month Ago.
Composite	469.28	+ 0.43	469.33	456.93
Indust	454.68	+ 0.04	455.99	444.99
NMS Comp	205.28	+ 0.15	205.14	199.67
NMS Inds	178.06	− 0.02	178.35	174.27

Amex Issues

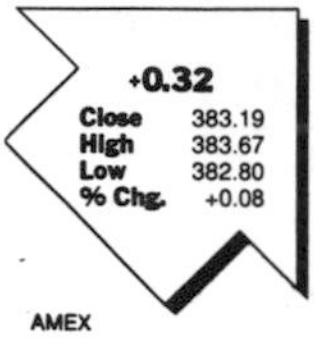

+0.32
Close 383.19
High 383.67
Low 382.80
% Chg. +0.08

AMEX

MARKET DIARY

	Yesterday	Prev. Day
Advanced	272	211
Declined	281	367
Unchanged	279	259
Total Issues	832	837
New Highs	34	21
New Lows	12	11

MOST ACTIVE: SHARE VOL.

	Vol. (100s)	Last	Chg.
DataPd	9558	10	−2¼
BAT	6365	12¾	...
Alza	5618	39⅜	+ 1⅜
Atari	5480	9⅞	+ ¾
TexAir	4315	19⅜	− ½
Thermd	3725	18	+ 1⅜
WangB	3659	5⅜	+ ⅛
Cross	3598	34¼	−3½
IntTlch	3353	4⅞	+ ⅜
FruitL	3280	15¾	+ ½
Amdhl	2758	15⅜	+ ⅛
ICH	2385	5½	+ ¼
BolrPh	2344	20½	− ⅛
ATTC wt	2206	1 3/16	...
Frd wt92	2077	1¾	...

CHANGES: UP

	Last	Chg.	Pct.
Versar	6⅝	+ 1	17.8
Nantuckln	9¼	+ 1⅜	17.5
BankBldg	5¾	+ ¾	15.0
IntlTelchg	4⅞	+ ⅝	14.7
AmTr-mob sc	12⅛	+ 1½	14.1
AmTr-chv sc	11⅜	+ 1⅜	13.8
WellsGard	5⅛	+ ½	10.8
Etz Lavud	5¼	+ ½	10.5
AlpineGrp	2¾	+ ¼	10.0
PrecsnAero	2¾	+ ¼	10.0
UnFoodsA	2⅞	+ ¼	9.5

CHANGES: DOWN

	Last	Chg.	Pct.
DataProd	10	− 2¼	18.4
Iroquois Bd	5⅜	− 1	15.7
HeritEntmnt	2¼	− ¼	10.0
CrossAT	34¼	− 3½	9.3
Harvey Gr	3⅛	− ¼	7.4
Firstcorp	4⅞	− ⅜	7.1
FurVault	3½	− ¼	6.7
LSB Ind	2⅛	− ⅛	5.6
GTI Corp	4⅜	− ¼	5.4
Tofutti	2¼	− ⅛	5.3

VOLUME COMPARISIONS

Day's sales	13,550,000
Previous day	12,300,000
Year ago	9,870,000
1989 to date	2,107,310,000
1988 to date	1,768,730,000

Other Measures

WILSHIRE

SANTA MONICA, Calif. (AP) — The Wilshire Associates Equity Index, the market value of NYSE, American and OTC issues, was $3,418.655 billion Thursday off $6.060 billion or 0.18 percent from Wednesday. A year ago the index was $2,646.085 billion.

UP-DOWN SHARE VOLUME

	Shares Advanced	Shares Declined
NYSE	65,388,270	69,297,290
AMEX	6,479,215	4,044,050
NASDAQ	59,498,200	34,482,403

VALUE LINE

NEW YORK (AP) — The Value Line Geometric Index of 1,685 NYSE, American and OTC stocks was 276.92 Thursday, up 0.04 points, or up 0.01 percent, from Wednesday. A year ago the index was 230.68. The Arithmetic Index, was 303.40 Thursday, up 0.09 points, or up 0.03 percent from Wednesday. A year ago was a 239.26.

THE WALL STREET JOURNAL

While *The New York Times* is very important, *The Wall Street Journal* is still the repository of all major financial news. For in-depth coverage of the world of money, there's nothing like the *Journal*.

Let's start by scanning the paper. Read the front page carefully, particularly the two lead articles, for an in-depth view of an important topic. Then look at "What's News" for the latest financial, national and international news. Sometimes the news is summarized in a brief paragraph; sometimes you'll be referred to a feature story within the paper. The second column from the right has glimpses of a particular topic—taxation, personnel, Washington wire or a particular industry—that changes daily.

Browse through the whole first section for domestic and international news. As with the *Times*, read the editorial pages in the back of the first section. The back page gives commentary on how presidential and congressional policies affect the financial community.

In 1988 the *Journal* expanded from two sections to three. The second new section, called "The Marketplace," allowed the *Journal* to cover more "soft" news—*i.e.,* items of interest to the financial community but not directly related to corporate goings-on or the stock market. You'll now see more articles on employee benefits, the law, data processing, the health industry and the like than ever before.

The third section, "Money & Investing," is where you'll find the hard business news. Three columns—"Your Money Matters," "Abreast of the Market" and "Heard on the Street"—focus on one particular financial instrument or one company. The cynics among us will say that if you read it here it's too late to make any money by following the column's advice. They may be right; it's sort of like being an armchair quarterback to run out and act on yesterday's news. However, even if you don't get any "hot" stock market tips, you'll read some interesting thoughts by industry movers and shakers that may help shape your investment strategy.

THE DOW JONES AVERAGES ®

High
Close
Low

Industrials

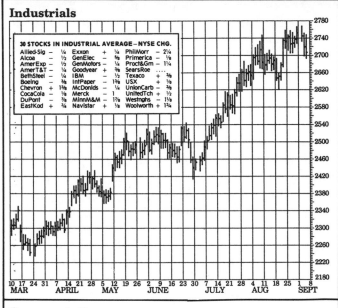

30 STOCKS IN INDUSTRIAL AVERAGE – NYSE CHG.

Allied-Sig	− ¼	Exxon	+ ¼	PhilMorr	− 2¼
Alcoa	− ½	GenElec	− ⅝	Primerica	− ⅛
AmerExp	− ½	GenMotors	− ¼	Proct&Gm	− 1¼
AmerT&T	− ¼	Goodyear	+ ⅜	SearsRoe	....
BethSteel	− ¼	IBM	− ½	Texaco	+ ⅜
Boeing	− ⅜	IntPaper	− 1⅜	USX	+ ⅛
Chevron	+ 1⅜	McDonlds	− ¼	UnionCarb	− ⅜
CocaCola	− ⅛	Merck	− 1	UnitedTch	+ ½
DuPont	− ⅞	MinnM&M	− 1⅞	Westnghs	− 1⅛
EastKod	+ ¾	Navistar	+ ⅛	Woolworth	+ 1¾

10 17 24 31 7 14 21 28 5 12 19 26 2 9 16 23 30 7 14 21 28 4 11 18 25 1 8
MAR   APRIL   MAY   JUNE   JULY   AUG   SEPT

Transportation

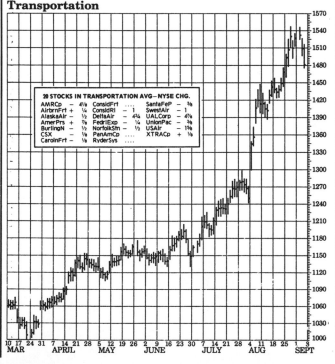

20 STOCKS IN TRANSPORTATION AVG – NYSE CHG.

AMRCp	− 4⅛	ConsidFrt	....	SantaFeP	− ⅜
AirbrnFrt	+ ¼	ConsidRl	− 1	SwestAir	− 1
AlaskaAir	− ½	DeltaAir	− 4¾	UALCorp	− 4⅞
AmerPrs	− ⅞	FedrlExp	− ¼	UnionPac	− ⅜
BurlingN	− ½	NorfolkStn	− ½	USAir	− 1⅝
CSX	− ⅛	PanAmCp	....	XTRACp	+ ⅛
CaroInFrt	− ⅛	RyderSys	....		

10 17 24 31 7 14 21 28 5 12 19 26 2 9 16 23 30 7 14 21 28 4 11 18 25 1 8
MAR   APRIL   MAY   JUNE   JULY   AUG   SEPT

Utilities

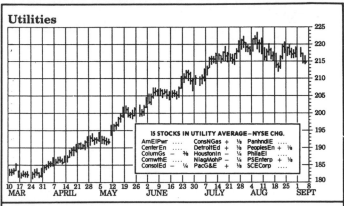

15 STOCKS IN UTILITY AVERAGE – NYSE CHG.

AmElPwr	....	ConsNGas + ⅛	PanhndlE ....
CenterEn	....	DetroitEd + ⅛	PeoplesEn + ⅛
ColumGs − ⅜		HoustonIn − ¼	PhilaEl ....
ComwthE	....	NiagMohP − ¼	PSEnterp + ⅛
ConsolEd − ¼		PacG&E + ⅛	SCECorp ....

```
10 17 24 31  7  14 21 28  5  12 19 26  2  9  16 23 30  7  14 21 28  4  11 18 25  1  8
MAR       APRIL        MAY        JUNE        JULY        AUG        SEPT
```

NYSE Volume

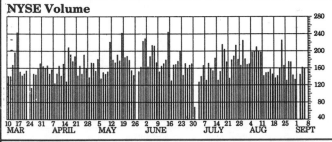

```
10 17 24 31  7  14 21 28  5  12 19 26  2  9  16 23 30  7  14 21 28  4  11 18 25  1  8
MAR       APRIL        MAY        JUNE        JULY        AUG        SEPT
```

Following are the Dow Jones averages of INDUSTRIAL, TRANSPORTATION and UTILITY stocks with the total sales of each group for the period indicated.

DATE	OPEN	10 AM	11 AM	12 NOON	1 PM	2 PM	3 PM	CLOSE	CH	%	HIGH*	LOW*	VOLUME
30 INDUSTRIALS													
Sep 7	2726.44	2726.63	2726.63	2721.12	2723.78	2723.40	2722.07	2706.88	− 12.91	− 0.47	2748.10	2692.06	21,035,500
Sep 6	2746.88	2722.07	2716.76	2707.45	2710.49	2710.68	2718.84	2719.79	− 24.89	− 0.91	2752.09	2697.95	22,992,400
Sep 5	2748.48	2571.71	2747.34	2754.56	2755.13	2742.21	2747.15	2744.68	− 7.41	− 0.27	2768.24	2731.76	18,315,300
Sep 1	2732.33	2735.75	2748.86	2756.08	2746.01	2751.71	2752.85	2752.09	+ 14.82	+ 0.54	2766.91	2726.82	16,862,200
Aug 31	2729.10	2730.24	2729.29	2729.29	2728.91	2727.39	2733.66	2737.27	+ 9.12	+ 0.33	2744.68	2717.90	17,127,000
20 TRANSPORTATION COS.													
Sep 7	1510.14	1506.40	1500.71	1496.09	1495.20	1495.02	1488.09	1480.97	− 27.74	− 1.84	1516.54	1474.93	5,863,700
Sep 6	1525.43	1518.14	1508.89	1502.13	1505.33	1504.80	1509.25	1508.71	− 23.30	− 1.52	1526.67	1495.91	5,309,100
Sep 5	1533.43	1535.03	1538.58	1538.94	1539.30	1532.72	1535.38	1532.01	+ 5.69	+ 0.37	1546.59	1524.18	5,159,200
Sep 1	1520.80	1519.20	1524.72	1527.03	1527.03	1528.27	1526.14	1526.32	+ 16.90	+ 1.12	1535.38	1512.09	5,439,500
Aug 31	1508.36	1517.78	1510.85	1506.58	1504.80	1504.45	1507.11	1509.42	− 20.10	− 1.31	1522.94	1491.64	8,897,300
15 UTILITIES													
Sep 7	215.86	215.73	215.79	215.73	215.61	215.48	215.17	214.66	− 0.25	− 0.12	216.61	214.10	3,738,300
Sep 6	217.05	215.98	215.42	215.10	214.85	214.85	215.42	214.91	− 2.33	− 1.07	217.43	214.35	3,746,500
Sep 5	218.12	217.87	217.74	217.93	218.00	217.18	217.30	217.24	− 1.38	− 0.63	219.06	216.23	3,808,200
Sep 1	216.80	216.93	217.87	218.44	217.93	218.56	218.31	218.62	+ 1.32	+ 0.61	219.25	216.11	3,922,400
Aug 31	217.18	217.81	217.74	217.24	216.93	216.86	216.74	217.30	+ 0.25	+ 0.12	218.37	215.92	2,288,600
65 STOCKS COMPOSITE AVERAGE													
Sep 7	1096.74	1095.83	1094.53	1092.20	1092.49	1092.28	1090.15	1084.81	− 9.51	− 0.87	1103.51	1079.76	30,637,500
Sep 6	1104.30	1097.75	1094.03	1090.19	1091.44	1091.36	1094.57	1094.32	− 12.48	− 1.13	1107.30	1086.14	32,048,000
Sep 5	1108.56	1109.47	1109.27	1111.06	1111.31	1106.39	1108.18	1106.80	− 1.21	− 0.11	1116.61	1101.46	27,282,700
Sep 1	1101.17	1101.63	1106.43	1108.93	1106.39	1108.35	1107.93	1108.01	+ 8.09	+ 0.74	1113.81	1097.45	26,224,100
Aug 31	1097.79	1100.67	1098.79	1097.45	1096.74	1096.29	1098.21	1099.92	− 2.54	− 0.23	1105.43	1090.57	28,312,900

Averages are compiled daily by using the following divisors: Industrials, 0.658; Transportation, 0.703; Utilities, 1.988; Composite, 2.995.

*Averages of the highs and lows reached at any time during the day on the New York Stock Exchange by the individual stocks.

STOCK MARKET DATA BANK 9/7/89

MAJOR INDEXES

HIGH	LOW	(12 MOS)	CLOSE	NET CHG	% CHG	12 MO CHG	% CHG	FROM 12/31	% CHG
DOW JONES AVERAGES									
2752.09	2038.58	30 Industrials	2706.88	− 12.91	− 0.47	+ 643.76	+31.20	+ 538.31	+ 24.82
1532.01	866.64	20 Transportation	x1480.97	− 27.74	− 1.84	+ 614.33	+70.89	+ 511.13	+ 52.70
221.64	178.52	15 Utilities	214.66	− 0.25	− 0.12	+ 34.60	+19.22	+ 28.38	+ 15.24
1108.01	773.69	65 Composite	x1084.81	− 9.51	− 0.87	+ 311.12	+40.21	+ 258.87	+ 31.34
331.70	248.19	Equity Mkt. Index	327.17	− 0.73	− 0.22	+ 76.71	+30.63	+ 66.43	+ 25.48
NEW YORK STOCK EXCHANGE									
196.37	148.96	Composite	193.78	− 0.40	− 0.21	+ 43.32	+28.79	+ 37.52	+ 24.01
235.86	178.73	Industrials	232.74	− 0.51	− 0.22	+ 51.99	+28.76	+ 43.32	+ 22.87
94.23	71.27	Utilities	92.32	− 0.14	− 0.15	+ 20.84	+29.16	+ 17.63	+ 23.60
212.37	133.83	Transportation	204.41	− 3.72	− 1.79	+ 70.58	+52.74	+ 57.81	+ 39.43
166.33	126.98	Finance	165.35	+ 0.16	+ 0.10	+ 32.19	+24.17	+ 37.16	+ 28.99
STANDARD & POOR'S INDEXES									
353.73	263.82	500 Index	348.35	− 0.89	− 0.25	+ 82.47	+31.02	+ 70.63	+ 25.43
405.27	302.84	Industrials	399.21	− 0.95	− 0.24	+ 94.54	+31.03	+ 77.95	+ 24.26
331.07	205.55	Transportation	319.01	− 6.17	− 1.90	+ 113.46	+55.20	+ 90.84	+ 39.81
143.25	108.93	Utilities	139.67	− 0.23	− 0.16	+ 30.26	+27.66	+ 27.03	+ 24.00
33.59	24.28	Financials	33.12	− 0.02	− 0.06	+ 7.40	+28.77	+ 8.63	+ 35.24
NASDAQ									
471.42	365.07	Composite	469.68	+ 0.43	+ 0.09	+ 89.95	+23.69	+ 88.30	+ 23.15
457.27	356.15	Industrials	454.68	+ 0.04	+ 0.01	+ 73.49	+19.28	+ 75.73	+ 19.98
543.32	421.05	Insurance	540.91	+ 2.54	+ 0.47	+ 113.42	+26.53	+ 111.77	+ 26.05
491.16	433.41	Banks	489.85	+ 1.24	+ 0.25	+ 37.69	+ 8.34	+ 54.54	+ 12.53
206.08	158.23	Nat. Mkt. Comp.	205.28	+ 0.15	+ 0.07	+ 41.09	+25.03	+ 39.63	+ 23.92
179.10	138.03	Nat. Mkt. Indus.	178.06	− 0.02	− 0.01	+ 30.73	+20.86	+ 30.64	+ 20.78
OTHERS									
384.53	285.37	Amex	383.19	+ 0.32	+ 0.08	+ 86.19	+29.02	+ 77.18	+ 25.22
278.69	223.04	Value-Line (geom.)	276.92	+ 0.04	+ 0.01	+ 46.24	+20.05	+ 44.24	+ 19.01
178.82	139.87	Russell 2000	178.43	+ 0.30	+ 0.17	+ 31.78	+21.67	+ 31.07	+ 21.08
3458.15	2610.87	Wilshire 5000	3418.66	− 6.06	− 0.18	+ 769.37	+29.04	+ 680.23	+ 24.84

MOST ACTIVE ISSUES

NYSE	VOLUME	CLOSE	CHANGE
Allergan	3,167,200	20¾	− 3¾
Upjohn Co	2,120,200	40⅞	+ ½
Genentech Inc	2,039,000	21⅛	+ 1¼
Goodyear Tire	1,993,100	57⅝	
Exxon Corp	1,881,800	44¼	+ ⅜
AMR Corp	1,741,500	82⅝	− 4⅜
Phillips Pete	1,583,100	27½	− ⅛
Texaco Inc	1,495,300	51	+ ⅜
Eastman Kod	1,467,800	49⅛	+ ¾
Gen Motors	1,383,500	50	− ⅛
First Penn	1,353,500	15⅝	
McDonald's	1,342,800	28¾	− ⅜
Chevron Corp	1,282,300	59⅛	+ 1½
AT&T	1,265,700	38⅞	− ¼
U S X Corp	1,264,200	34⅞	+ ¼
NASDAQ NMS			
M C I Comm	4,187,500	40¼	+ 1
Applied Biosys	1,619,700	24¾	− 3¾
First Executive	1,516,600	13½	+ ½
Offshr Logist	1,262,100	8 5/16	+ 1/16
Seagate Tech	1,155,000	12⅞	+ ⅛
Greenwich	1,149,700	4⅞	+ ¾
Intel Corp	1,017,100	29¾	− ¼
Apple Cmptr	1,016,900	44¾	
Sensormatic	996,100	13¼	+ ⅝
Integ Device	953,600	10⅝	+ ⅛
Chips & Techn	941,500	20¾	− ¾
D S C Comm	910,600	14⅛	+ ⅛
Safecard Svcs	872,800	6	+ ¼
AMEX			
Dataproducts	956,300	10	− 2¼
B.A.T Indus.adr	636,500	12¾	
Alza Corp	561,800	39⅜	+ 1⅝
Atari Corp	548,000	9⅞	+ ¾
Texas Air Corp	431,500	19⅝	− ½

DIARIES

NYSE	THUR	WED	WK AGO
Issues traded	1,996	1,980	1,983
Advances	713	433	801
Declines	714	1,091	672
Unchanged	569	456	510
New highs	76	42	77
New lows	18	22	11
zAdv vol (000)	66,304	37,839	72,002
zDecl vol (000)	69,298	108,283	49.319
zTotal vol (000)	160,160	161,800	143,420
Closing tick[1]	-330	−169	+110
Closing trin[2]	1.04	1.14	.82
zBlock trades	3,412	3,079	3,069
NASDAQ			
Issues traded	4,377	4,376	4,378
Advances	1,008	783	1,027
Declines	929	1,168	827
Unchanged	2,440	2,425	2,524
New highs	125	97	133
New lows	51	52	32
Adv vol (000)	58,609	54,928	52,113
Decl vol (000)	33,325	44,673	27,071
Total vol (000)	133,997	136,432	117,756
Block trades	2,090	1,839	1,801
AMEX			
Issues traded	832	837	847
Advances	272	211	313
Declines	281	367	243
Unchanged	279	259	291
New highs	34	21	31
New lows	12	11	8
zAdv vol (000)	6,516	3,010	4,649
zDecl vol (000)	4,027	6,323	5,826
zTotal vol (000)	13,550	12,300	13,170
Comp vol (000)	16,243	14,869	15,580
zBlock trades	241	190	235

PRICE PERCENTAGE GAINERS . . .

NYSE	CLOSE	CHANGE	% CHG
Tiffany & Co	60⅜	+ 6⅛	+ 11.3
Lomas Fncl	3¾	+ ⅜	+ 11.1
Intelogic Tra	3	+ ¼	+ 9.1
Galveston-Hou	3⅜	+ ¼	+ 8.0
Fischbach	18⅝	+ 1⅜	+ 8.0
Firstfed Finl	23¼	+ 1⅝	+ 7.5
Permian.pf	5⅜	+ ⅜	+ 7.5
Datapoint	5½	+ ⅜	+ 7.3
Duke Rlty Inc	5¾	+ ⅜	+ 7.0
Natl Svc Indus	29½	+ 1⅞	+ 6.8
Tultex Corp	12	+ ¾	+ 6.7
Stoneridge Res	10⅛	+ ⅝	+ 6.6
Valero $2.06pf	36½	+ 2¼	+ 6.6
Genentech Inc	21⅛	+ 1¼	+ 6.3
Valero Energy	16¾	+ 1	+ 6.3
SPX Corp	35⅞	+ 2⅛	+ 6.3
Unvl Med Buildg	2⅛	+ ⅛	+ 6.3
Floating Point	2⅛	+ ⅛	+ 6.3
Public Svc NH	4½	+ ¼	+ 5.9
Worldcorp Inc	13⅜	+ ¾	+ 5.9
NASDAQ NMS			
Jetborne Intl	2⅝	+ 9/16	+ 27.3
Intl Hldg Cap	19	+ 4	+ 26.7
Am Pioneer	2¾	+ ½	+ 22.2
Greenwich	4⅞	+ ¾	+ 18.2
Jaco Electro	4⅜	+ ⅝	+ 16.7
Codenoll Tech	5¾	+ ¾	+ 15.0
Trimedyne Inc	8¾	+ 1⅛	+ 14.8
St. Ives Labs	11	+ 1⅜	+ 14.3
Cinn Micrwv	7⅜	+ ⅞	+ 13.5
Crown Andrsn	5¼	+ ⅝	+ 13.5
Eastco Ind Sfty	4¼	+ ½	+ 13.3
Southeastrn Sav	4¼	+ ½	+ 13.3
Sierra RE 1984	4¼	+ ½	+ 13.3
Reuter Inc	9¼	+ 1	+ 12.1
AMEX			
Versar Inc	6⅝	+ 1	+ 17.8
Nantucket Ind	9¼	+ 1⅜	+ 17.5
Bk Bldg & Equip	5¾	+ ¾	+ 15.0
Intl Telechrge	4⅞	+ ⅝	+ 14.7
Wells-Gardner	5⅛	+ ½	+ 10.8

AND LOSERS

NYSE	CLOSE	CHANGE	% CHG
Goldome	3⅝	− ¾	− 17.1
MohascoCorp	21¼	− 4	− 15.8
Allergan	20¾	− 3¾	− 15.3
ImperialAmer	3¾	− ⅜	− 9.1
RadiceCorp	3⅞	− ⅜	− 8.8
SysCenter	20¾	− 1¾	− 7.8
Data-Design	5⅞	− ½	− 7.8
ProlerIntl	23¾	− 1⅞	− 7.3
AileenInc	3⅜	− ¼	− 6.9
CaltonInc	1⅞	− ⅛	− 6.3
FnclSantaBar	2	− ⅛	− 5.9
PrimeCmptr	10⅛	− ⅝	− 5.8
EquitableRESh	8⅜	− ½	− 5.6
DeltaAirLines	75¼	− 4¼	− 5.3
AMRCorp	82⅝	− 4⅜	− 5.0
WesternUnBpf	7⅛	− ⅜	− 5.0
CntrywdMtg	4¾	− ¼	− 5.0
VestronInc	2⅜	− ⅛	− 5.0
CircuitCitySt	22⅜	− 1⅛	− 4.8
TidewaterInc	9⅞	− ½	− 4.8
NASDAQ NMS			
PortsOfCall	1⅜	− ¾	− 35.3
LexingtnPrec	1⅞	− ⅜	− 16.7
Varitronic	10¼	− 1⅞	− 15.5
AppliedBiosys	24¾	− 3¾	− 13.2
PhoenixAmer	3 11/16	− 9/16	− 13.2
ParlexCorp	3½	− ½	− 12.5
ElectronicTele	4¾	− ⅝	− 11.6
EastexEnergy	2	− ¼	− 11.1
SierraRE1983	6	− ¾	− 11.1
1stWoburn	6¼	− ¾	− 10.7
CmptrAutomat	2½	− ¼	− 9.1
RossCosmetics	3⅛	− 5/16	− 9.1
AmConsmrPd	7¾	− ¾	− 8.8
BenihanaNatl	2⅝	− ¼	− 8.7
AMEX			
Dataproducts	10	− 2¼	− 18.4
IroquoisBrands	5⅜	− 1	− 15.7
HeritageEntmt	2¼	− ¼	− 10.0
Cross(AT)Co	34¼	− 3½	− 9.3
HarveyGroup	3⅛	− ¼	− 7.4

VOLUME PERCENTAGE LEADERS

NYSE	VOL	% DIF	CLOSE	CHANGE
SeagullEnergy	198,700	1418.9	20⅛	+ ⅛
IpalcoEnterp	504,300	1042.9	x24⅛	− ⅛
Tiffany&Co	482,200	1010.7	60⅜	+ 6⅛
SysCenter	183,200	978.4	20¾	− 1¾
FirstPenn	1,353,500	819.6	15⅝	
StoneridgeRes	120,600	813.4	10⅛	+ ⅝
NevadaPower	219,100	734.4	22¼	− ¼
GenentechInc	2,039,000	716.0	21⅛	+ 1¼
KysorIndu	46,400	686.7	15	
OxfordIndus	45,000	627.1	12⅜	+ ⅛
Jamesway	424,000	604.3	10¾	+ ⅛
ThomasIndus	57,700	597.3	19⅝	
VulcanMat	155,200	567.8	46⅛	− ½
Cypress	974,200	534.6	11½	− ¼
GoodyearTire	1,993,100	526.5	57⅝	
DesotoInc	130,600	513.8	40¾	+ 1
PepBoys	722,800	504.7	12⅞	− ⅝
Allergan	3,167,200	a492.7	20¾	− 3¾
WhitehallCorp	56,900	487.0	17	+ ⅛
GiantGroup	73,400	464.6	20⅛	− ⅛

Common stocks of more than $5 a share with average volume over 65 trading days of at least 5,000 shares.
a – has traded fewer than 65 days on any exchange.

NASDAQ NMS	VOL	% DIF	CLOSE	CHANGE
NewBrunsScie	338,700	4450.6	7¾	+ ¼
WolhnLumber	173,900	1972.2	19¾	+ ¾
SuperRiteFd	275,200	1816.4	26¼	+ ⅛
SecurityBncp	148,500	1170.4	22½	+ 1⅛
AppliedBiosys	1,619,700	987.9	24¾	− 3¾
MarcorResorts	66,900	925.6	8⅛	+ ⅜
OffshrLogist	1,262,100	806.3	8 5/16	+ 1/16
QuarexIndus	48,400	806.0	7	+ ⅝
SafecardSvcs	872,800	729.0	6	+ ¼
Foster(L.B.)A	193,600	698.1	5¼	
AmericanMag	84,200	683.5	6⅜	+ ⅜
IntegDevice	953,600	663.8	10⅝	+ ⅛
ArgonautGroup	90,100	660.9	66	+ 1½
AlcoHlthSvc	56,700	628.5	24¾	− 2
PeoplesSavBk	51,300	609.2	8½	+ ¼
ElanCorp	611,000	607.3	11½	− ⅞
AMEX				
Cross(AT)Co	359,800	1443.5	34¼	− 3½
MooreMedical	103,400	1292.0	14⅝	+ ⅞
NorexAmer	72,800	1170.3	7¼	+ ⅜
Dataproducts	956,300	1028.8	10	− 2¼
Thermedics	372,500	844.6	18	+ 1⅜

BREAKDOWN OF TRADING IN NYSE STOCKS

BY MARKET	Thur	Wed	WK AGO
New York	160,160,000	161,800,000	143,420,000
Midwest	11,687,300	10,001,900	10,986,200
Pacific	6,068,100	5,964,300	5,581,200
NASD	9,274,230	11,308,850	5,902,850
Phila	2,723,100	3,311,300	2,611,400
Boston	3,011,500	3,261,900	2,954,300
Cincinnati	943,000	1,011,700	662,900
Instinet	216,200	148,100	233,800
Composite	194,083,430	196,808,050	172,352,650

·The net difference of the number of stocks closing higher than their previous trade from those closing lower. NYSE trading only.
x-Ex-dividend of Union Pacific Corp. 55 cents lowered the Transportation average 0.89. This lowered the Composite average 0.21.
z-NYSE or Amex only.

½-HOURLY	Thur	Wed	WK AGO
9:30-10		31,680,000	24,180,000
10-10:30	15,880,000	17,140,000	15,570,000
10:30-11	14,880,000	14,900,000	13,740,000
11-11:30	12,670,000	11,850,000	9,550,000
11:30-12	13,230,000	14,170,000	10,130,000
12-12:30	9,140,000	10,320,000	9,200,000
12:30-1	8,020,000	6,270,000	6,950,000
1-1:30	7,210,000	10,010,000	5,890,000
1:30-2	7,080,000	6,910,000	5,820,000
2-2:30	8,810,000	8,030,000	8,490,000
2:30-3	9,520,000	9,640,000	8,820,000
3-3:30	14,740,000	9,500,000	6,070,000
3:30-4	14,910,000	11,360,000	19,010,000

The "must read" columns in this section are the "Dow Jones Averages" (see pages 30-31) and the "Stock Market Data Bank" (see pages 32-33). The Dow Jones Averages give you a six-month overview of the thirty stocks that compose the industrials, twenty stocks in the transportation industry and fifteen utility stocks. The "NYSE (New York Stock Exchange) Volume" you see is important; while the DJI might change very little on a given day, a high volume of buying and selling might indicate that the market is volatile, although the pluses and minuses could cancel each other out.

The "Stock Market Data Bank" tells you how the major indexes closed for the day. Each major index looks at its own portfolio of large companies' performances, so you'll want to follow each one. Note that the Dow Jones Averages, New York Stock Exchange, Standard & Poor's Indexes and NASDAQ are the biggies, with AMEX, Value-Line, Russell and Wilshire also quoted. These latter four indices are all based on the same stock market data bank as all the others. What these represent for individual investors are some choices about how to analyze and track data. Value-Line, Russell and Wilshire are all backed up by newsletters for which investors pay annual fees of hundreds of dollars to get expert market research and opinion on how and when to invest. Many investors like the convenience and security of having the advice of investment industry gurus at their fingertips.

The data-bank Diaries also gives you the number of stocks that advanced and declined over the day. From that you can get a ratio. For example: 4 to 1 advances over declines means that for every one stock that advanced, four declined. This should also be reflected in the total volume of advances and declines.

Last, you'll want to review the Most Active Issues and Price Percentage Gainers and Losers every day. This will give you a perspective of what individual companies are trading most actively on the market, as will the Volume Percentage Leaders. This will tell you that something's going on, but you'll have to do more research to find out just what that thing is.

Chapter 4

DAILY DIGGING— ELECTRONICALLY

The number of sources of information has grown so rapidly that who but the professional can absorb it all? If it seems that in the last few years professionals have outperformed individuals, have individuals somehow become less intelligent recently? Not at all, for the answer may lie in how professionals get their information. For the most part, they rely increasingly on their computers for up-to-the-minute news.

In the last few years a number of relatively affordable and user-friendly electronic data bases have become available, granting investors access to a wide variety of information, including:

- model stock portfolios

You may want to put together your own portfolio of favorite stocks and ask the computer to analyze how it performed over a specified time period. This gives you a chance to try your hand at investing without actually putting money into the stock market until you're ready. You can ask the computer to monitor the ups and downs of your model (simulated) port-folio indefinitely. When you're pleased with the results of your investing acumen, you can then take the plunge, for real, into the stock market. The computer tells you:

• best- and worst-ranked stocks with buy and sell recommendations

• stock-performance predictions and ratings

• search and historical capabilities on individual stocks

One of the things a computer does best is research. Tirelessly and accurately it will search for information about a company, industry or any specific aspect of business operations—such as marketing U.S. pharmaceuticals in Canada—in a fraction of the time that it takes to do the same task by hand. It can do the same for any particular stock, including researching what publications printed news of the stock, and providing abstracts of that news. Among the things one can find are:

• NYSE, AMEX, NASDAQ and CBOE (Chicago Board of Exchange) quotes for stocks, options, market indices, mutual fund and corporate bond quotes

• currency rates and index rates

• backgrounds on thousands of corporations

• news clips on people, companies and products

In fact, there's so much available that it's hard to fathom exactly what you, the individual investor, need to know to facilitate your decision-making process. Whatever you do, your electronic daily digging should build on the foundation provided by your perusal of the printed word—*i.e., The New York Times* and *The Wall Street Journal.*

Will the personal computer (PC) ever replace the daily newspaper as the source of financial news? I'd like to think that the answer is no, but Sears and IBM are betting big money, through a joint venture called Prodigy,™ that one day every household will use a PC to get the news, go shopping, make travel plans, buy stocks and more.

Prodigy is an on-line service that is being mass-marketed right now. Starter kits are available in computer stores and bookstores, and they are easy to install. You simply hook your personal computer to the phone line, using a modem; it is through this phone link-up that all the outside information and services become available. Prodigy is very easy to use and has something for everyone in the family—from financial data to travel bargains, at-home shopping, encyclopedias and even up-to-the-minute news. You move from one topic to another using a list of familiar "jump words." This Sears-IBM venture is a big gamble and a big investment for both companies, but they're betting that Prodigy's low cost ($9.95 a month) and ease of use will attract a wide market.

Just how ready is the average person for this kind of service? Let's take a look at the technology available today to a computer-literate individual.

Getting Started

The components required for electronic searching are:

- a personal computer

- modem

- communications software

- an on-line data-base service

For most people with their own computers, whether in the home or at work, the cost of adding communications capability is around $200, not a high price to launch yourself into the computer age.

Perhaps the easiest place to start is with the public utilities that offer extensive information services along with E-mail and electronic conferencing. E-mail and electronic conferencing are ways of communicating with other people who have personal computers and modems. You can send and receive messages to people in different time zones, different parts of the world or right next door. Messages can be about any topic

(E-mail) or structured around specific topics or interests (conferencing). With conferences you can read all the messages about a particular subject, then decide if you want to join the discussion. Once you join you'll receive all new messages and are free to send messages. With E-mail and conferencing you can send private notes to just one person, a distribution list or all conference members.

E-mail and computer-conferencing networks are springing up all over the place. The two you should know about are: CompuServe,™ the granddaddy of information providers, which has close to 400,000 users, second in the world only to France's Minitel;™ and The Source,™ a similar service with roughly 60,000 members. Both offer a sort of supermarket of electronic services and access to on-line data bases for stock quotes, commodities information, major market and industry indices and more. Both allow you to profile an individual company and to analyze its performance over the last several years. In addition to financial information, they offer a wide array of business, leisure, educational and shopping services. For the price of a nominal start-up fee and per-minute charges for connect time you can begin to follow the market segments that interest you. Both CompuServe and The Source keep you up to date on services for investors and often send fact sheets on how to use a particular service.

More Sophisticated Services

"I need timely information" is the demand of investors everywhere, and on-line services are happy to oblige. After all, one of the problems with the daily newspaper is that it presents yesterday's news, which tells you about the past, but does not provide the current information that will help you make decisions today.

Generally, the more "timely" the on-line information is, the more costly it will be for you to get it. Here's how some of the more popular providers stack up on timeliness:

- NEXIS™ (from Mead Central Data)

NEXIS is a news and business service that has 8 million full-text articles from more than 125 magazines that are updated daily. This gives you access to a tremendous number of sources. But since the updates are daily, what do you gain over reading the newspaper? You get to read many articles pertaining to what interests you. The time lag, though, can be considerable. *The New York Times* is updated within twenty-four hours; *The Washington Post, The Los Angeles Times* and *Financial Times* usually within two days. Though you may be getting news that's several days old, you are at least getting a good deal of depth.

- DIALOG™

DIALOG contains many of the same files as NEXIS but adds on BUSINESSWIRE and REUTERS, both of which are updated every fifteen minutes. This is pretty impressive; you can really stay on top of the news with this. BANKNEWS, providing the full text of *American Banker*, is also a service of DIALOG, giving you today's newspaper on-line.

- Global Report™ (from Citibank)

Global Report has been marketed as so user-friendly that even harried senior managers with little computer experience can learn to use it in less than twenty-four hours! Using most of the same sources as NEXIS and DIALOG, Citibank adds an emphasis on international financial news, including the latest rates for 150 currencies, forex (foreign exchange) rates from international banks and specific recommendations and advice on hedging (linking two or more securities into one investment position to reduce risk).

- Dow Jones News Retrieval™

Dow Jones News Retrieval updates its data base every ninety seconds throughout the day, giving you the most current information you'll get on-line. When you see a TV image of an arbitrageur with a telephone glued to each ear and his eyes riveted to a computer terminal, chances are he's using Dow Jones Retrieval. There are times, particularly when dealing with significant news events of publicly traded companies, that current information is critical. News of mergers, acquisitions or an earnings statement fall into this category.

The Costs

The catch to all this wealth of information is the cost—financial talk isn't cheap. There can be many ways to spend your money on electronic digging, including:

- one-time registration fee
- monthly service charge
- per-minute charge
- per-item charge
- value-added service charge
- search fee
- fees for printed text
- storage fees

You shouldn't be scared off by the multiplicity of fees. You can learn to use your on-line services efficiently. You can learn to do cost-effective searching and get the information to enhance your financial acumen. Some ways to spend the least amount of money while getting optimal results are:

- Use the services at off-peak hours, usually after 6 P.M.

- Plan the search before you log on, including having the file and item names written down for quick reference.

- Download results to a printer so that you can study the material later, at your leisure.

- Shop around for the on-line service that has exactly what you want.

- Be aware of promotional opportunities.

Some on-line services allow you to try a new product for free during the initial period. Also, when you buy a product, perhaps the modem or the telecommunications software, you may be offered a registration fee free of charge.

- Take advantage of yearly subscription rates rather than paying on a monthly basis, since it's usually cheaper.

Is This for You?

It's a big jump from the morning newspaper to getting your news electronically. On-line news can help investors increase their profits by getting the latest financial news as quickly as possible. It can tell you what's happening in the latest multibillion-dollar merger or in the DJI at any moment and give you instant access and analysis of a company. You get the newsgathering power of virtually every wire service at your fingertips.

Why isn't *everyone* plugged into his or her PC at all times? It will probably take another decade for people to be totally comfortable using their computers to gather the news, and on-line news may never replace the satisfaction that comes when you linger over your morning paper with a cup of hot coffee, slowly absorbing and mulling over what you read. On-line news is fast, and you have to like to move at a fast pace to get the most out of it. Perhaps using an on-line data base on a trial basis is the best way to assess whether this method is right for you.

For more information . . .

For more information about on-line electronic services, an excellent resource is *The Complete Handbook of Personal Computer Communications*, by Alfred Glossbrenner (St. Martin's Press, 1985). Or you can write to:

"Computer-Aided Investing: Introduction and Resources"
Investor Support Systems, Inc.
26 Pinecrest Drive
Hastings-on-Hudson, NY 10706

Chapter 5

STEPS TO A FINANCIAL PLAN

F inancial planning is like going to the dentist. You know you should do it, but you put it off even if you're in considerable pain. When the hurt gets unbearable, either with a toothache or a financial emergency, you go begrudgingly to the dentist with your toothache or to a financial planner with your cash pinch, elevated tax burden or lightened investment. That's when you recognize that prevention is the best medicine, after all.

Many of us assume, incorrectly, that since we know how much debt we have, that our accountant does our taxes, that our lawyer once did our will and that we have a pension at work, we have a financial plan. We also assume, incorrectly, that simple budgeting is financial planning, and that anything more is unnecessarily restrictive.

On the contrary, a financial plan finds dollars, directs dollars more productively to our priorities and maximizes current corporate benefits and taxes so that we can enjoy greater financial peace of mind, all within the constraints of tax law.

Step One: Budgets

If the concept of financial planning seems alien to you, let's get back on more familiar terrain—budgets. Businesses have budgets, as do individuals, and they serve similar functions. Because they are more detailed and formal, corporate budgets are clearly superior to the typically informal budgets drawn up by individuals. More important, business budgets must consider profitability, long-and short-term potential for growth, available resources, cash flow, marketing and the like, not all of which pertain to personal budgets. Yet there really is more to financial planning for individuals than isolated and informally derived budgets.

According to Dr. Herbert Froehlich, a senior vice-president of PCC Advisory Corporation in Hartsdale, New York, budgeting and financial planning differ substantially. Budgeting deals with day-to-day cash flow, while financial planning deals with:

- improving cash flow, not just living with it

- making investments productive, not just being a passive observer of the scene

- planning for tax containment, while recognizing the impact of this concern on the performance of investments

- funding college and meeting retirement objectives, given available resources

- insuring the continuity of income during disability so as to preserve the level of investments and cash flow

- securing assets and a life-style in the event of an untimely death

Financial planning focuses on securing and improving your life-style rather than just living from day to day and hoping for the best. Financial fitness is the end result of planning. In part, it is determined by checking your level of:

- net worth (assets minus liabilities)

Resistance to Financial Planning

If making a financial plan is such a good thing, why don't more people do it? Dr. Froehlich points out that there are many obstacles that stand in the way, including:

• fear that our darkest assumptions will come true, rather than basing our decisions on facts

• inertia or laziness that makes us keep on doing what we're doing rather than trying a fresh approach

• hoarding (shortsightedness), which narrows our focus and turns us away from examining future possibilities, perhaps keeping our money in low-yield but familiar accounts

• fear of losing control; planning involves a process that will shape behavior, and if we don't like that fenced-in feeling we will not surrender control, even if it furthers our financial goals. We tend neither to accumulate assets nor show responsibility toward our families. One obvious example is the failure to develop wills and acquire proper insurance

• hidden agendas between spouses; for example, if they can't agree on other things, agreement on a financial plan is highly unlikely

• uncertainty about professional planners themselves; this is a new professional specialty, and an unregulated one; if you seek professional help, make sure you choose one of the 12,000 who are registered with the SEC. (There are nearly 300,000 people in the United States who call themselves financial planners!)

This index indicates one's overall capacity to respond to financial emergencies due to increases in expenses or decreases in income.

• liquidity of assets

Liquidity refers to the actual level of assets readily convertible into cash with which emergencies are met. There needs to be a proper balance among investments so as to gain long-term advantages, while maintaining sufficient liquidity.

- cash flow (income less expenses)

Cash flow reflects the money available for savings or being drawn out of savings or credit to meet expenses.

Assessing all of this gives us a start in developing a financial plan, and, together with other factors, helps determine whether:

a. you will outlive income or not (in other words, will you have enough income to see you through old age with the medical and maintenance expenses you may incur?)

b. inflation will erode positive cash flow

c. additional insurance is required

d. you can retire early

e. college funding may need to be supplemented from other sources

Step Two: Setting Goals and Priorities

In order for your budgeting and financial planning to make any sense, you need to start with a specific objective or question that is critical to you:

- I want to do a little better than my parents. How can I do that?

- How can I retire at age 56?

- Can I reduce my taxes?

- Should I start a pension plan at my place of business?

These questions can be the basis of a financial plan because their answers may lead to other questions. In fact, if these questions are properly answered, other questions could find answers, too. Before you know it, you feel that you've made progress and you sense a usable set of priorities being developed.

Questions really can't be totally answered out of context. Froehlich gives the example of a thirty-four-year-old self-employed musician who approached him at a seminar and said: "I've got one hundred forty thousand dollars that I just inherited. What should I do with it now?" The potential client's first impulse was to spend some, invest some in munis and put the balance in CD's and a few stocks. Froehlich told this fellow that he could not answer his questions without knowing his goals, his other resources and income, his tax bracket and his liabilities. Basically, this free-lancer with variable income and no corporate benefits needed help. Here's the answer that the two arrived at together:

1. Purchase a disability plan to protect against loss of income.

2. Purchase $250,000 worth of insurance on top of $25,000 he already had to help secure the family's life-style and reduce some outstanding debt.

3. Establish a pension plan and deposit 20 percent of earnings into it, using the inherited money. This takes care of some of the money and gains a tax deduction to boot.

4. Maintain $12,000 in liquid form for emergencies.

5. Use $40,000 of the inheritance as a 25 percent down payment on a condominium or house; the resulting mortgage will be tax deductible, and, if the house appreciates 10 percent per year, $16,000 more would be added to his net worth annually.

The preceding example suggests the many productive results that came from one financial question. Froehlich is quick to point out that the question of where to put the money might have been answered differently by a stockbroker, an insurance salesperson or a realtor rather than a financial planner. The ultimate goal, of course, of the financial planning process is to bring the person's or couple's resources together with his, her or their objectives.

Step Three: Developing a Strategy

Based upon your objectives, and with such facts as income, expenses, liabilities, future dollar demands, tax structure, the prevailing investment climate and risk tolerance, personal and company insurance policy, the type of retirement plan and its funding and one's will in hand, a financial planner can orchestrate a program that moves you toward financial fitness.

The key elements of a plan should cover:

- tax planning
- educational funding
- cash flow
- insurance protection
- investment structuring
- retirement
- estate taxes and distribution

All of these components, discussed in this book, will interrelate and be personalized. That's the whole idea—financial fitness for yourself and your family. Most questions should have answers, even those not covered in the written plan, including:

- Should I refinance my house or move?

- Should I quit my job?

- Should I send my children to a private college or state school?

- Will I be able to support my dependent parents?

Of course, changes in your life may require you to draw up a new financial plan several years down the road. Your first plan is a solid foundation for moving smoothly in any new direction.

If You Want Professional Financial Help

Finding a financial planner can be tricky, because anyone can call him- or herself a "financial planner." Luckily, there are guidelines you can use when shopping around.

Several national groups offer certification for professionals who complete courses on financial planning. You should look for someone who is a:

- CFP (Certified Financial Planner)
- CFC (Chartered Financial Consultant)
- CFM (Chartered Financial Manager)

Sometimes, an attorney or certified public accountant may be qualified, even without these specific credentials, by virtue of their professional experience. Overall there are roughly 400,000 people calling themselves "financial planners" and "financial consultants." Of this number, only 20,000 are registered with the Securities and Exchange Commission. Experts say that it's preferable to deal with a financial planner who is a SEC licensee.

One of the most important questions to ask of a prospective financial planner is, "How are you paid for your services?" The options are: fee only, commission only and fee plus commission. Those paid on a commission-only basis make their money on the sale of products, such as life insurance, about which they're giving advice, so they have an interest in pushing products where they'll make the highest commission. Fee-only planners may charge costs that you can't afford. A mix of fee-only and commission-only works best for most people.

It's also wise to find a financial planner who will work with you on a long-term basis. As you and your family move through different life cycles, your needs will change.

Chapter **6**

HOLDING ON TO YOUR ASSETS

Now that you've seen how financial planning can bring your objectives and resources together to achieve a more productive result, we're going to explore a few related strategies and simple steps to help you toward financial savvy and security.

Let's assume that you've taken the basic steps outlined in the previous chapter. You've set your goals based on a realistic understanding of your resources; you've done tax planning and investment diversification. The next step is risk management—protecting yourself against loss of the objectives that you have established.

Certainly risk management for large companies is a very complicated subject, far beyond the scope of this book. However, most of us as individuals engage in risk management, albeit unknowingly. We do it when we purchase car insurance, take out a homeowner's policy or buy/receive group life and/or disability insurance offered by our company. Dealing with risk should be part of our personal financial fitness schedule. It may be an unpleasant task, but to secure our own and our family's future we have to ask ourselves:

- How can I keep my assets from being reduced because of taxes?

- What will happen if I'm unable to work or if I die before my children are grown?

- Will the integrity of the family's assets be protected if income is lost or expenses rise unexpectedly?

Life Insurance

Essential to most financial plans is some form of life insurance. Put simply there are two kinds: term and whole life.

- Term

Like car or homeowner's insurance, it allows you to rent protection. When the year is up you renew your option and rent it again, except at an increased cost. It is useful for temporary needs.

- Whole Life

This is protection you own. It is much more expensive than term insurance, but it is used for permanent needs throughout your life. It has cash buildup, its costs are level and could be "self-sustaining" after only seven years.

You buy life insurance to replace your income if you die, so that if you earned $50,000 a year your family will have close to $50,000 a year to replace the lost income. If your family's expenses are greater than the lost income, will your spouse's income or drawing on years of savings be enough? Many people carry insurance only until their children are grown, then drop it, thereby forgetting about the value of this same insurance to provide the basis for a sounder retirement benefit or paying estate taxes.

Life insurance can be used as an alternative pension option and possibly increase the retirement benefit 20 percent, while adding flexibility to an inflexible situation. At retirement just consider taking the maximum employee option of your pension and use your insurance to provide your spouse's benefit. Whether your spouse lives or not, using insurance maximizes your available cash, is a hedge against inflation and provides a death benefit to a third person not available with a corporate pension.

Many people use insurance policies creatively as their needs change. They purchase low-cost term insurance to begin with, convert it to a higher whole or universal life policy, borrow against the cash value for business or personal use or establish an insurance trust to save on estate taxes.

Securitization

"Securitization" or "asset-backed lending" are terms that we hear with increasing frequency nowadays. They refer to loans that are secured by an asset, or collateral. The principal groups of secured loans for consumers are:

- Liquid assets

This means such things as checking and savings accounts, certificates of deposit, the cash value of life insurance and various securities.

- Cars, trailers, mobile homes and boats

These items constitute titled collateral. Since these types of assets involve a greater risk of loss to the lender because the item remains in the owner's possession and repossessing it can be costly, this is considered a risky loan.

- First and second mortgages

Many people use their homes as collateral against a loan. Home-equity loans are extremely popular. They allow home-owners to translate the equity built up by their home's appreciation, usually 8 to 12 percent each year, into cash for a variety of business and personal uses.

Secured or "asset-backed" loans have gotten more attention in the last several years in both the consumer and commercial markets. Lenders feel more confident lending larger amounts, at longer maturities and at lower interest rates on loans that are backed by an assignable asset than with only the customer's good credit rating. However, a good credit rating never hurt anyone.

Unsecured Loans

If you are unable to secure a loan from a bank or governmental agency such as the SBA (Small Business Administration), there are other options for you—unsecured loans. Such loans are made based on the creditworthiness of the borrower. Their chief advantage over secured loans is that no collateral is required. For many people these are highly desirable loans.

In addition to completing an application, the only other paper work necessary is a promissory note—a legal instrument, or proof of debt, that records the agreement between the borrower and the lender.

ARE YOU CREDITWORTHY?

Generally, lenders look at these three factors when judging creditworthiness: credit history, job history and residence background.

1. Credit History

Sometimes people who pay their bills on time and who have carefully avoided bad debts still may be labeled as a "risk." They may never know that such a label is sticking to them until they have occasion to apply for a credit card or loan. How can this happen?

Unfortunately, in this increasingly sophisticated world, many things can go wrong, and will. Here are some scenarios that can cause one to end up with a bad credit rating:

- Computer error

Through someone's mistake and no fault of your own, you may be erroneously labeled a bad risk.

- A dispute over billing

If you've ever withheld funds, either fully or partially, in disagreement over a charge billed to a credit card, this may show as nonpayment.

- Too much credit

You may want to take advantage of a new credit-card opportunity but may be denied because the sum of all the credit available to you, even if you don't use it, exceeds what the lender feels you can afford to pay.

- Self-employment

Entrepreneurs and free-lancers, even with steady incomes, make lenders very nervous. The best thing is to establish credit if and when you have a full-time job, then pay your bills on time when you're self-employed.

- Bad history

If you ever had a dry spell or, worse, had to declare bankruptcy, this will obviously hurt your creditworthiness. However, you can reestablish credit by taking out a small loan and repaying it on time, without fail.

2. Stable Job History

Lenders like to see that people have established patterns in their employment, specifically, patterns of staying in one place. People who jump from job to job, spending a year or less in each place, represent risks to lenders because such people are likely to experience fluctuations in income which, in turn, could jeopardize their ability to make payments due on loans.

3. Residence Background

The same holds true when it comes to residence patterns. Generally, lenders like to see at least two years in one place.

HOW TO FIND OUT IF YOU'RE A CREDIT RISK

If you're thinking of applying for a loan or just want to have a record of your creditworthiness, write to:

> TRW, Inc.
> P.O. Box 271
> Parsippany, NJ 07054

Include: your name (include Jr. or Sr., if applicable); spouse's name; present and previous addresses; city, state, and ZIP code; Social Security number.

If your application for credit has been declined by TRW within thirty days, enclose the notice to that effect with your letter and this information will be given to you at no charge. If not, send a check for $15.00, payable to TRW, with your letter.

Leverage

Put simply, you can use a borrowed dollar to buy two dollars' worth of benefit. Many people who buy stocks use leverage to buy more stocks. For example: You buy a stock for $1. It jumps in price to $2. You're legally allowed to use half the leverage between $1 and $2, or 50 cents, to buy more stock. To be concrete, let's say you bought 200 shares in ABC Corporation for $1 per share. One month later, ABC's price soars to $2 per share. If you sold the stock you'd have $400. On paper, and in reality, you've made a profit of $200. However, you like ABC and want to invest in more stock. Federal law allows you to invest up to 50 percent of your paper profit ($100 in this case). This is called "buying on margin," a phrase usually associated with the Great Depression of 1929, when investors were able to purchase stock with as little as 10 or 20 percent as a down payment. The 50 percent margin rule that exists now protects you from being financially devastated during a severe market downturn, but still allows you a good degree of leverage.

Leverage can be used outside stock market circles as well.

For example, if your house is worth $400,000 and you borrow $100,000 to purchase a second house, you now own two pieces of property. You used the first as leverage to gain the second.

Leveraging does several things for you financially:

- It allows you to invest in more assets.

- It may allow you to translate taxable dollars into tax-free or tax-deferred dollars by moving them to another asset.

Leveraging for individuals gives you some idea of how a leveraged buyout (LBO) works for corporations. A company uses a relatively small amount of cash to repurchase the outstanding shares of stock at a premium. LBO's will be discussed in more detail in Chapter 9.

Helping Your Assets Grow

There may be times when you need cash to make an investment that seems right to you: perhaps establishing a small business, purchasing a piece of real estate or some shares of stock.

If securing a loan from a bank or governmental agency, as we described above, doesn't seem possible, there are other avenues you may want to investigate. They are:

- Credit cards

You may use your business or personal credit cards to pay business expenses or to obtain cash for working capital. Entrepreneurs have been known to finance businesses using six or seven cards. Be careful to pay at least the minimum amount each month; with a good payment history your credit limits should increase.

- Leasing equipment

Leasing equipment such as computers, copiers and fax machines may be a source of financing in which the leasing company retains ownership and title to the assets as collateral.

Overall, the lease payments may total more than the purchase price, but leasing rather than buying frees cash for other items.

- Life insurance

This was covered previously in this chapter. Remember that you can borrow against policies that have cash value. Keep in mind that the loan subtracts from the worth of the policy. Should the policy be needed, only the balance of the policy will be paid.

- Supplier credit

Suppliers you deal with often permit small businesses to buy inventory or equipment on an open account for thirty to ninety days. You can use the "float," the time between when you receive money and the time you have to pay it to the supplier, to your advantage.

- Personal loans/other people's money (OPM)

Personal loans or other people's money may be either single-payment or installment loans. Single-payment loans are usually due in thirty, sixty or ninety days. Installment loans are paid in monthly portions and have a maturity of one to five years. For small amounts of cash, these may be easier to get than a business loan. Banks may or may not require that the loan be secured with collateral.

- Retained earnings (or internal financing)

Don't overlook your own savings or profits from past ventures as a vehicle to move into new, growing operations.

Managing your cash flow, protecting your income and your family, maintaining your life-style and your good credit rating, acquiring assets and watching them grow—these are all part of sound financial planning.

Chapter 7

UNDERSTANDING CORPORATE ANNUAL REPORTS

here are many ways of learning about a company's financial performance. You can consult the major financial encyclopedias such as *Moody's* and *Standard & Poor's*. You can subscribe to hundreds of financial publications. You can obtain analyses from the major brokerage houses. One of the best ways is to obtain a company's annual report. It can be procured easily from a brokerage house, a bank or directly from the company. Of course, if you are a stockbroker, you will receive it automatically.

Reading an annual report can be a daunting experience. Many of them are boring, and some are hard to understand. However, the better annual reports are excellent resources.

How to go about this will of course to some extent depend on your objectives. You may want to read an annual report as a student and for general interest. You might be an investor or potential investor. Or you could be a job-seeker. In our discussion we shall try to cover reasonably all the bases.

For illustrative purposes we have chosen the 1988 annual report of the Bristol-Myers Company, a diversified drug company that won a number of awards for the excellence of its reports and which ranks seventy-ninth on the Fortune 500 list.

The Bristol-Myers report devotes twenty-eight of its sixty-four pages to an article entitled, "America Comes of Age," which deals with that ever-increasing segment of our population, older Americans. Bristol-Myers is interested in older Americans because many of them spend a larger amount of money on health-care products than do younger people.

Closely related to this special report is a "Programs of Public Interest" section, which tells of research grants and programs and positions Bristol-Myers as a good corporate citizen interested in high-tech medical research, investing in education and being an equal-opportunity employer. From these two segments of the report one can deduce that this company has a broad range of interests with particular emphasis on developing and marketing medical and pharmaceutical products throughout the world.

Next we turn to the letter from the chairman and chief executive officer. Probably a great many people from the various divisions have contributed to the writing and editing of this letter. It summarizes important trends for the stockholders about research, sales, profits, personnel and new ventures. Product lines are described, as are leadership positions in various market segments and the complexities resulting from doing business as a global company.

All the key financial data are right there in the chairman's letter:

- growth in sales and earnings
- net earnings and earnings per share
- dividends
- profit margins
- domestic and international sales growth
- thumbnail sketches of the major product lines

From this letter you should get a feeling about the direction in which this company is headed. Obviously, it wants to project itself in the best possible light, so you want to read between the lines for any statements indicating stagnant growth or a downhill course. A final thing you should glean from the chairman's letter is an idea of who the key executives in the company are. This may be read in conjunction with the list of officers and their positions, which in most cases appears at the end of the annual report.

Financial Highlights

Bristol-Myers places these right on its inside front cover (see page 60). This gives you an overview of all the basic data:

- sales
- earnings
- cash position (or cash flow, as it is commonly called)
- number of employees

However, in order to understand what's really happening, you need additional, more detailed information.

These are the real guts of the report, the "Consolidated Statements of Earnings and Retained Earnings" (also called the "Profit and Loss Statement," or P&L) and the "Consolidated Balance Sheet" (see pages 61-62).

Key things to look for in the P&L are:

- **Net sales.** These should increase every year.

- **Expenses.** Unfortunately, these must also increase. Try to compare the percentage increases of sales and of expenses. While there's no hard and fast rule for making the comparison between these two percentages, it's safe to say that if the percentage of expenses increases more than the percentage of sales, then the company may be in trouble.

- **Net earnings.** This is probably the most important figure in the annual report. This is sales minus expenses minus taxes. Examine trends in absolutes and as a percent of sales. Basically, what you want to do is to compare this year's net earnings with those of the previous year. Note that in this case net earnings increased from $709.6 million to $829.0 million, a gain of 17 percent. That's a pretty impressive number

(dollars in millions except per share amounts)	1988	1987	% Change
Net sales	$5,972.5	$5,401.2	11
Earnings before income taxes	$1,285.3	$1,117.5	15
As a percent of sales	21.5%	20.7%	
Net earnings	$ 829.0	$ 709.6	17
As a percent of sales	13.9%	13.1%	
Return on stockholders' equity	24.5%	23.4%	
Earnings per common share	$ 2.88	$ 2.47	17
Dividends per common share	1.68	1.40	20
Cash, cash equivalents, time deposits and			
marketable securities	$1,709.9	$1,577.6	8
Working capital...........................	2,401.8	2,164.3	11
Capital expenditures	252.3	190.0	33
Book value per common share	12.31	11.21	10
Number of employees......................	35,200	34,100	
Stockholders of record	58,104	54,074	

because it represents real growth in earnings—that is, after taxes have been calculated.

The balance sheet reflects the company's financial position as of the end of the years shown. It is sometimes called the "Statement of Financial Position." To understand it, keep these definitions in mind:

• **Assets.** These are properties that are owned and have monetary value. The main ones are usually cash, securities, receivables (monies earned from sales but not yet actually received), inventory, plant and equipment.

• **Liabilities.** These are amounts owed to outsiders, such as bank loans, accounts payable, taxes payable and long-term debt such as bonds.

• **Stockholders' equity.** This is the interest of the owners of the enterprise.

Consolidated Statements of
Earnings and Retained Earnings

Year Ended December 31,

(in millions of dollars except per share amounts)	1988	1987	1986
Earnings Net Sales.	**$5,972.5**	**$5,401.2**	**$4,835.9**
Expenses:			
Cost of products sold.	1,803.6	1,678.8	1,515.2
Marketing, selling and administrative.	1,606.5	1,464.0	1,303.0
Advertising and product promotion	978.8	918.7	820.3
Research and development.	394.1	341.7	311.1
Other.	(95.8)	(119.5)	(44.1)
	4,687.2	4,283.7	3,905.5
Earnings Before Income Taxes	1,285.3	1,117.5	930.4
Provision for income taxes	456.3	407.9	340.9
Net Earnings.	$ 829.0	$ 709.6	$ 589.5
Earnings Per Common Share	$2.88	$2.47	$2.07
Retained Earnings Retained Earnings, January 1.	$3,010.8	$2,703.3	$2,414.4
Net earnings.	829.0	709.6	589.5
	3,839.8	3,412.9	3,003.9
Less dividends.	483.8	402.1	300.6
Retained Earnings, December 31	$3,356.0	$3,010.8	$2,703.3

These three elements are connected by a fundamental relationship called the accounting equation, as follows:

$$assets = liabilities + stockholders'\ equity$$

Now, let's look at the Bristol-Myers balance sheet in a little more detail. First we have the Current Assets: cash, marketable securities, inventory and receivables. These are the factors that show various degrees of liquidity—that is, the ability to meet financial obligations quickly and easily. The ratio between current assets and current liabilities is called the current ratio. For B-M this is 3.1 ($3,566 divided by $1,164), an excellent ratio. A company with a small ratio might be headed for trouble. Of course, for the purpose of making a more sophisticated analysis, we might have to examine other con-

		December 31,		
(in millions of dollars)		1988	1987	1986

Assets

Current Assets:

	1988	1987	1986
Cash and cash equivalents	$1,186.2	$ 353.4	$ 493.0
Time deposits	130.8	641.8	619.0
Marketable securities.	392.9	582.4	80.2
Receivables, net of allowances.	946.2	865.9	759.3
Inventories	688.6	617.9	615.0
Prepaid expenses.	221.1	202.3	192.1
Total Current Assets.	3,565.8	3,263.7	2,758.6
Property, Plant and Equipment — net.	1,249.1	1,141.9	1,070.0
Other Assets	173.6	143.8	165.3
Excess of cost over net tangible assets received in			
business acquisitions	201.2	182.6	189.1
	$5,189.7	$4,732.0	$4,183.0

Liabilities

Current Liabilities:

	1988	1987	1986
Short-term borrowings	$ 173.3	$ 223.4	$ 230.5
Accounts payable.	335.8	275.8	252.0
Accrued expenses	519.3	449.8	374.1
U.S. and foreign income taxes payable	135.6	150.4	158.6
Total Current Liabilities	1,164.0	1,099.4	1,015.2
Other Liabilities	263.5	193.0	174.5
Long-Term Debt	215.2	210.3	157.7
Total Liabilities	1,642.7	1,502.7	1,347.4

Stockholders' Equity

	1988	1987	1986
Preferred stock, $2 convertible series: Authorized			
10,000,000 shares; issued 81,730 in 1988, 95,782			
in 1987 and 123,689 in 1986, liquidation value of			
$50 per share	.1	.1	.2
Common stock, par value of $.10 per share:			
Authorized 750,000,000 shares; issued			
289,632,360 in 1988, 287,851,825 in 1987 and			
143,117,706 in 1986.	29.0	28.8	143.1
Capital in excess of par value of stock	312.7	275.8	137.4
Cumulative translation adjustments	(77.8)	(84.2)	(147.3)
Retained earnings	3,356.0	3,010.8	2,703.3
	3,620.0	3,231.3	2,836.7
Less cost of treasury stock — 1,885,512 common shares			
in 1988, 218,512 in 1987 and 96,756 in 1986.	73.0	2.0	1.1
Total Stockholders' Equity	3,547.0	3,229.3	2,835.6
	$5,189.7	$4,732.0	$4,183.0

siderations, such as the mix of current assets, valuation and prevalent ratios in the industry. (*Valuation* refers to how one sets the value of an asset—*e.g.,* at the market price or at the price you paid for it. *Prevalent ratio* refers to the ratios that hold

62

for a particular industry so that current ratios of competitors can be compared.)

Next you will note the line called "Property, Plant and Equipment—Net." This is sometimes called "fixed assets." The "net" means net after the deduction of depreciation. It is difficult to make judgments on this item without knowing much more about the industry and the company, but you can notice immediately that this business is not capital intensive, meaning that it doesn't have to invest heavily in new plants and equipment to keep it moving along. Imagine generating $6 billion in sales with only $1.2 billion of fixed assets! That's spending only a relatively small amount of money on factories and equipment to generate a whole lot of cash.

In the "Liabilities" section, one is struck by the fact that this company has only $215 million of long-term debt. That's an impressive figure because long-term debt is what the company has to borrow for a period of five years or more to finance its operation, sort of like an individual having to get a twenty-year mortgage to finance home ownership. For a company with more than $6 billion in annual revenue, $215 million in long-term debt is considered a small sum, indicating that the company either finances capital expansion through operating revenues or is very conservative about taking on debt.

The "Stockholders' Equity" section of the balance sheet tends to get quite technical because of the various classes of stock found in many companies, but there really is no need for the average reader to get involved with these details. Suffice it to say that common stocks are those shares of the company that are traded publicly on an exchange such as the New York Stock Exchange or American Stock Exchange. Preferred stocks, like common stocks, are securities that represent part ownership of a corporation. They are described as "preferred" because they grant the first right, before common stock, to any money the corporation has available to pay out in dividends. The important thing to note is that the total stockholders' equity, or net worth, is $3.5 billion. This is also called *book value*. Note in the "Financial Highlights" section that, expressed per common share, this comes to $12.31. For a going concern and a successful company, this figure is always much less than the market price because historical costs are fixed, while current trading prices are higher. You can find in the financial pages of your newspaper that in mid-1989 the market price was about four times as high—that is, approximately $48.

The next page in the annual report contains the "Consolidated Statement of Cash Flows." This shows how cash was generated and how it was used. One way of gaining a better understanding of what this statement tells us is to extract a few key figures, calculate a few percentages and put them in a little table:

Sources of Cash	$ (millions)	%
From operating activities	980.6	68
From investing activities	416.2	29
From stock options and warrants exercised	37.1	3
Effect of exchange rate on cash	2.5	—
	1436.4	100

Uses of Cash		
Dividends	483.8	34
Increase in cash position	832.8	58
Other	119.8	8
	1436.4	100

This tells us several very interesting things.

First, that 68 percent of the cash was generated from operations, a very good relationship, because a large amount of income was generated by an ongoing revenue stream, as opposed to selling a building, which is a one-time source of revenue.

Next, note that only 34 percent of the cash generated was used to pay dividends, because that cash was being generated and only about one-third of it was used for distribution. The rest is available for other purposes. This is a conservative and sensible policy.

Examined together with the relationship of dividends to earnings, which was 58 percent (calculated by dividing $1.68 by $2.88, numbers found in the Financial Highlights section), this tells us that a conservative policy is being followed of plowing a large part of cash and earnings into the business for future growth rather than taking a "quick buck" approach.

Financial Review

You're done with the most difficult parts of the study of the annual report, so now you can relax a little bit and take a different view of things. The "Financial Review" section gives you a largely self-explanatory discussion plus ten years of trend-watching in graphic form.

First let's take a look at the key figures—sales, earnings and earnings margins (see page 66).

The graphs, text and ten-year summary all show strong long-term and short-term trends. An increase in earnings margins results in earnings increases that exceed the sales increases—something you would like to see in a successful business. You can calculate a net earnings margin of 8 percent of 1979 compared to 14 percent for 1988. The average, or compound annual growth rates were 15 percent for earnings and 9 percent for sales, as mentioned in the text of the report; both are more than respectable numbers.

Now, let's look at the three big expense categories (see page 67).

Note that the first two—"Marketing, Selling and Administrative Expenses" and "Advertising and Product Promotion Expenses"—increased at rates comparable with the sales increases. The percentage of sales ratios therefore remained more or less steady at approximately 27 percent and 17 percent, respectively. On the other hand, research increased more steeply, and the percentage of sales ratio went from 3.7 per-

Sales

$ Millions

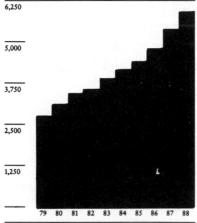

Net Earnings

$ Millions

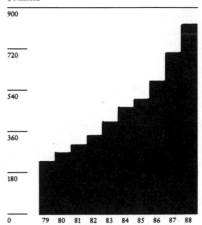

Net Earnings Margins

% of Sales

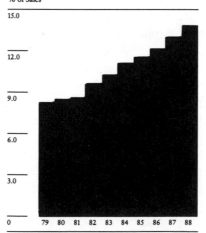

Marketing, Selling and Administrative Expenses

$ Millions

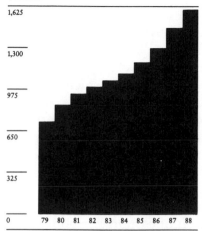

	79	80	81	82	83	84	85	86	87	88

% of Sales
26.4 27.2 27.2 27.9 26.8 26.4 26.8 26.9 27.1 26.9

Advertising and Product Promotion Expenses

$ Millions

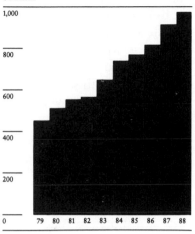

	79	80	81	82	83	84	85	86	87	88

% of Sales
16.6 16.2 15.9 15.8 16.6 17.8 17.5 17.0 17.0 16.4

Research and Development Expenses

$ Millions

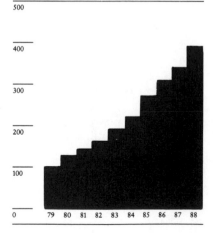

	79	80	81	82	83	84	85	86	87	88

% of Sales
3.7 4.1 4.1 4.6 4.9 5.3 6.1 6.4 6.3 6.6

67

cent in 1979 to 6.6 percent in 1988. This is what might be expected from one of the largest pharmaceutical companies in the world, which seeks to enhance its position primarily through research.

Before we leave the various analyses of items related to the profit-and-loss statement, let's ask ourselves one last question: Since, as we have just seen, the increase in earnings margin did not come from reductions in the three major expense categories, from where did it come? The answer, which we can glean from the ten-year summary, is reductions in the cost-of-goods-sold ratio. The cost-of-goods-sold ratio works like this: If something cost $40 to produce and it was sold for $100, the cost-of-goods-sold ratio is 40 percent. B-M's cost-of-goods-sold as a percentage of sales declined from 38 percent in 1979 to 30 percent in 1988.

Before we leave the financial analysis we should mention one last indicator that is rarely shown in corporate reports but which the financial community considers very important: the price-to-earnings ratio (P/E). This is simply the market price divided by the per-share earnings. For Bristol-Myers at the end of 1988 this was about 15 (45 divided by $2.88). The P/E ratio increases or decreases as investors show willingness to accept a share of stock according to how they view its future prospects. Companies with positive potential growth have high P/E's, and the opposite holds true for a company with poorly perceived prospects.

The Seal of Approval

Near the end of the annual report there should be a statement by the accounting firm responsible for an independent review of this work. This statement should be in accordance with SEC (Securities and Exchange Commission) disclosure rules, the IRS (Internal Revenue Service) and the FASB (Financial Accounting Standards Board).

You get the feeling that this is probably a rubber stamp of

approval for all the work done by the company's internal and external auditing, accounting and tax-planning teams. There are certain situations of which you should be aware. If the auditor's statement says "these results are subject to" or says nothing about GAAP (Generally Accepted Accounting Principles), it could mean that there are serious financial implications for the company. Always check for anything that indicates the auditor's uncertainty about the future of the company. In the case of Bristol-Myers, though, note that Price Waterhouse gives its stamp of approval without qualification.

We have reviewed one particular annual report, but what we learned here can be applied to any annual report. Of course, an annual report reflects a great deal about the company that produces it—from the corporation's style and how it wants to present itself to what it thinks is important for its shareholders to know. Doing a careful reading of a company's annual report is an excellent way to understand what that company is all about, both financially and in an overall sense. As you gain experience from reading annual reports from different companies, you should get a good feel about each company's style, current performance, what it values and its future direction.

Chapter 8

FINANCIAL INSTITUTIONS: AS THE WALLS COME TUMBLING DOWN

The financial world has changed so drastically in the last twenty years that it's scarcely recognizable today. From a dozen or so small banking houses that conducted their business quietly, we now have a few global giants.

Perhaps the best real-life illustration of how financial institutions have changed is to make a study of the emergence of a brand-new entity, called by a variety of names, that merged the following companies: Shearson Hayden Stone, Kuhn Loeb & Lehman, E.F. Hutton and American Express. Those mergers signaled the end of a variety of corporate cultures, market segments and personal customer services and created a mega-giant that could be all things to all people. What were once small banking houses have now become a five-legged creature that does retail brokerage (for the individual investor creating a stock, bond or fund portfolio), money management, real estate, stock trading (on the major stock exchanges) and investment banking, all backed by an enormous operations division.

Shearson Lehman Brothers

Peter Cohen, the forty-two-year-old chairman of Shearson Lehman Hutton, is known as an impatient and ambitious man who goes after what he wants and usually gets it. He started his career in 1969 at CBWL-Hayden Stone, a small brokerage firm. Several years later, in 1973, the firm changed its name to Shearson Hayden Stone and set itself on the road to empire-building.

In 1981 Shearson was sold to American Express by its chief, Sanford Weill, who saw the opportunity to make Shearson a more muscular presence—a global house. The acquisition legitimized Shearson because American Express, with its common stock and debt as a large reservoir of financing power, enabled Cohen to build the business quickly. Cohen needed the power of American Express's vast ability to borrow to make transactions quickly and at a bargain price.

In 1984, Shearson-American Express, headed by Cohen, swallowed up Kuhn Loeb Lehman. The takeover propelled Shearson into the world of investment banking. Cohen was moving toward becoming a major force in mergers and acquisitions, the takeover of one company by another. By having American Express's ability to finance debt because of its tremendous borrowing capacity, and Lehman Brothers's expertise at evaluating companies as being financially attractive or not as takeover candidates, Cohen had all the elements he needed to be a major player in this exciting but very risky game.

However, there were several other things he had to do to reach his goal. One was to let Nippon Life, a Japanese insurance company, acquire a 13 percent stake in Shearson for $530 million, fueling the acquisition machine with cash. Shearson and Nippon Life agreed that the latter's stake could grow to 33 percent without Shearson's further approval. (This threshold is important for two reasons: First, it allows Shearson to tap into a large source of funds provided by Nippon Life. Second, it means that a foreign company has a significant minority shareholder's stake in a highly visible and important American financial institution.) The other major move was the public stock offering of 18 percent of Shearson. The Nippon move and the stock offering gave Cohen the cash to shop to a merchant banker's heart's content.

What is the ultimate goal of giving these pieces of the company away? To challenge the unquestioned dominance of Merrill-Lynch as America's biggest securities firm. Shearson is now a close, rather a distant, number two. While Shearson has been aggressive, Merrill-Lynch has been relatively stagnant.

To achieve his goal of parity with Merrill-Lynch, Cohen had to make yet another acquisition, that of the house of Hutton. He needed Hutton for its money-management operations. Its relatively weak but improvable investment banking and trading operations were another plus. Consider, also, Shearson's mammoth data-processing facility in Manhattan, completed in 1986. The facility would give Cohen the capacity for 100,000 trades a day—nearly 70 percent more than he had without it.

The Fall of the House of Hutton

This is not a pretty story. Greed, selfishness and mismanagement that included criminality plagued this once-proud old-line brokerage firm and brought it to its knees. We'll explore some of the acts committed by Hutton—some illegal and some that were just bad business decisions—that weakened it, making it a prime target for being taken over by a company with better cash flow and sounder management. How could this happen?

• **1985**—Hutton entered a guilty plea to a check-kiting scheme. (Check kiting is something that nearly anyone who is a little short of cash might do. Let's say you have two accounts—a checking account and a savings account. You promised someone) you'd write him or her a check and you do, even though you know there aren't enough funds in your account to cover the amount. In the meantime, you collect interest on the savings account for a few more days, then withdraw the money and deposit it in the checking account and hope that everyone will think that the original check, the one that "bounced," was just a mistake. Check kiting is bad when anyone does it, but when executives in a financial company do it routinely and intentionally to generate extra income, it's a big no-no, not to mention a federal crime.) From 1980 to 1982 Hutton managers intentionally overdrew the firm's checking accounts for a day or two to earn additional interest, to the tune of $4 million. The firm pleaded guilty and was indicted for 2,000 counts of mail and wire fraud.

• **1985**—Hutton was accused by state regulators of selling units of limited partnerships without necessary approvals.

• **1986**—Although Hutton lost $90 million in 1986, and profits had been slipping since 1981, its officers continued spending extravagant sums on trips, lavish parties and other frills.

• **1987**—A money-laundering scheme in Rhode Island was revealed, and federal prosecutors recommended indictments. Following the advice of E.F. Hutton's legal counsel, C.E.O. Robert Fomon decided to plead guilty in federal court as a way of avoiding indictments against some of Hutton's senior executives.

• **1989**—Shearson Lehman Hutton's Boston chief, James von Germeten, was fired and two other senior executives resigned following an investigation into the company's accounting practices. Their mistake? Overstating the first three quarters of earnings for 1988.

Many in the financial industry expressed shock and surprise when law-enforcement officials caught up with E.F. Hutton. Is what they did any worse than what goes on at other brokerage houses and investment banks? The answer is "yes" and "no."

Yes, there are certain companies with bad reputations that seem to operate constantly in the gray area between criminality and questionable business practices. Then there are those companies with the sterling reputations—such as Salomon Brothers, Goldman Sachs and Morgan Stanley—that are protective of their outstanding images.

What was particularly unfortunate about the fall of Hutton is that, while the bigwigs at the top threw themselves a nonstop party, the little people at the bottom got hurt. One of the first things that Cohen of Shearson did when he acquired Hutton was to close its back office. Six thousand workers lost their jobs, mostly in operations, capital stock markets and investment banking. The head-rolling continued. In 1988, 1,000 more Hutton employees were terminated. The Hutton board of directors treated itself a lot better than its employees. It voted itself a $2.5 million package of retirement benefits before the party was finally over.

Given this mess and this history, why did Shearson Lehman want to gobble up Hutton?

Shearson Lehman Hutton

In the late 1960s and early 1970s, E.F. Hutton was what one would expect a brokerage house to be. Rather staid, in 1970 it had revenues of $85 million and a staff of only 1,275 account executives, or salespeople (as compared to Shearson's much larger staff of roughly 6,500 salespeople). In 1972 the company went public, meaning that it offered stock and became listed as a publicly traded company on the New York Stock Exchange.

Between 1972 and 1986 Hutton's market share of the brokerage trade grew from 2.9 percent to 7.6 percent. It opened 200 new offices nationwide to handle the increase in business. Revenues were rising faster than costs. Through 1975 profits grew 22 percent a year and net worth increased by 21 percent.

The trouble started in 1975, when the SEC deregulated brokerage commissions. That signaled the beginning of a new business—discount brokering, with commissions as low as $25 a trade. Hutton's high-flying brokers, with their 40 percent commissions (versus an industry norm of 30 percent), were given a clear signal, which they cheerfully ignored.

On the investment banking front, Hutton never did manage to compete successfully with rivals Morgan Stanley and Goldman Sachs. Instead of developing a strategy for deal-making, the firm used a hit-or-miss approach. Most of the deals it tried missed. A good example of Hutton's lack of savvy and success in investment banking was its issuing in 1982 of a tax-free corporate note with a floating (variable depending on fluctuations in the prime rate) interest rate. Because of a misreading of market conditions, Hutton wound up paying out to bond holders $55 million in excess of what it had projected.

Mismanagement and overspending continued through the late 1970s and into the early 1980s. A comprehensive plan for $46 million in savings by 1988—based on reducing the firm's twelve regional offices to four, realigning the back-office systems, dropping unproductive lines of business, eliminating 550 marketing jobs and reducing commissions—was dealt a mortal blow by the October 19, 1987, stock market crash. The firm was left with only two options—an injection of capital or a sale.

After the crash, Wall Street was in turmoil and nervous about the faltering E.F. Hutton. Major banks reduced their lines of credit to the firm. Investors clamored for the sale of $1 billion in short-term notes to raise cash. The price of Hutton's stock fell to $15 a share; it had been $35 only two weeks earlier. The sharks smelled blood and circled the carcass.

Cohen saw his opportunity to acquire Hutton and therefore become competitive with Merrill Lynch. His chief fear was that Merrill would beat him to the punch and snap up Hutton at a bargain basement price. So Cohen moved quickly. Although he had offered Hutton $50 per share of stock just one year earlier and had been rebuffed on December 1, 1987, E.F. Hutton's board agreed to be acquired by Shearson for

$29 a share. Though the price came close to $1 billion, this was far less than it would have been at $50 a share.

The Results

The creation of Shearson Lehman Hutton produced a five-legged global banker with:

- retail brokerage
- money management and real estate
- stock trading
- investment banking
- a transaction processing center

Since the merger the firm has been in the top five in mergers and acquisitions, including deals with Federated Stores, Stop & Shop, Eastman Kodak and Koppers. Two of its star executives have developed a new financial instrument—the unbundled stock, which is a mechanism that slices each share of preferred stock into three separate securites, each one having a different yield and tax treatment. Four companies— American Express, Dow Jones, Pfizer and Sara Lee—are using unbundled stocks as a way to increase interest payments to bond holders and to make investments in such stock attractive.

Activities such as this point to a worldwide structure of a handful of full-service global giants: Shearson Lehman Hutton American Express, First Boston and Merrill Lynch in the United States; Nomura, Daiwa, Nikko and Yamaichi in Japan. What the disappearance of the small, old-line firms will mean, ultimately, remains to be seen. The demise of small, specialized firms in favor of the mega-giants reflects and is part of the trend toward depersonalization in practically all service industries. It's becoming increasingly difficult for small firms—whether they are insurance agents, banks with only one branch, local real estate offices and even the corner grocery store—to compete against the resources and the economies of scale that the big guys enjoy at the expense of the little guys.

How's It Doing?

Did Shearson's acquisitions make it the global powerhouse that Cohen intended? In 1988 the company took a financial beating. Brokers' yearly commissions dropped from a 1987 average of $250,000 to $195,000 in 1988. The firm's mergers-and-acquisitions business results were mixed. It earned $300 million but lost $200 million in potential fees as sharper and more able investment bankers landed some really big deals that could have gone to Shearson if it had been more astute. Experts say there will be more layoffs.

Being a global concern means being expert and versatile in all areas of finance. Many in the business community feel that Shearson has spread itself too thin in businesses it doesn't know much about, particularly mergers and acquisitions. It's a matter of principle. Should a company or individual try to be everything to everybody, or stick to what it does well? We can look to Shearson in the next few years for answers to that question.

Goldman Sachs, often an archrival of Shearson in the mergers-and-acquisitions business, stands in stark contrast in terms of corporate style. Goldman Sachs is relatively small; with only 4,000 employees (Shearson has 42,000!), it tries to be competitive and to be the best, which it often is. Rather than catering to small companies and individuals with small amounts to invest, Goldman Sachs deals with large corporations with deep pockets. *Forbes* magazine estimated that Goldman Sachs traders account for 5 percent of the daily volume on the New York Stock Exchange and 25 percent of trades of 10,000 or more shares. Goldman Sachs is a class act, pays excellent salaries and bonuses, demands and gets hard work from its staff and continues to be a small, focused and powerful group of outstanding investment bankers. The next decade should be an interesting time for the concept of specialization versus size to be tried out in the marketplace.

Chapter 9

THE NEW WRINKLE: LEVERAGED BUYOUTS (LBO'S)

Wouldn't we all like to have our cake and eat it, too? It's a childhood dream—to consume something, yet have it left over. Many grown-ups, especially in the business and corporate world, don't relinquish that dream. We're always looking for a deal that's "too good to be true," something that offers endless rewards.

In most cases a deal that's "too good to be true" isn't. There's a catch to it, some hidden factor that makes the offering less attractive than it appears at first blush. Not so with the leveraged buyout, the grown-up's dream come true.

A Quick History

The 1980s will be remembered as a time when a lot of business owners who didn't have much money acted as if they did. Thanks to their investment bankers, led by the pioneering money people at Drexel Burnham Lambert and Kohlberg

Kravis Roberts, they were able to transact deals, called leveraged buyouts.

Investment bankers who put together LBO's are a breed apart from most other bankers. If your image of a banker is a conservative type in a pin-striped suit who very carefully manages Aunt Millie's trust account, the investment bankers at Drexel Burnham and KKR may seem as if they come from another planet. Aggressive, brash, working long hours and even around the clock when they're putting the finishing touches on a mega-deal, their goal is to bring a company to its knees so that their client, the buyer, can acquire the company, either in a friendly or a hostile takeover. They're not shy about making money. Firms such as Drexel Burnham and KKR make huge fees once they've consummated a deal. Here's how the mechanism of their favorite type of deal, a leveraged buyout, works:

1. The buyer, either an individual or group, decides to make a publicly owned company private.

2. The takeover is accomplished by using the company's assets as collateral.

3. The buyers, usually top management and some outside investors, borrow against the company's assets to buy all of its outstanding stock.

4. Nonrated bonds known as "junk bonds" are issued to manage the debt.

5. The stockholders receive cash and bonds for tendering their shares.

6. After an LBO the company is in private hands.

7. The new owners then take steps to reduce the debt to manageable levels by selling off assets, streamlining operations and cutting staff.

8. Often, stock is reissued to the public soon after the LBO.

There are several important things to note here. The notion of what constitutes an "asset" has been redefined. Companies are not necessarily using factories or inventory as collateral, but unused borrowing potential. Most notable of all, virtually everyone involved in an LBO makes a great deal of money: the new owners of the company, the banks that provide the financing, the financial advisers and the stockholders who surrender their shares.

Although the mechanism has been available for years, LBO's were a 1980s phenomenon. Government statistics show that about 1,400 companies worth more than $130 billion went private through leveraged buyouts since 1983, including Borg-Warner, Burlington Industries, Eckerd Holdings, Beatrice Corporation, Safeway, Macy's, Mary Kay Corporation and Revco.

Can LBO's really be this simple? Can management just decide to turn unused borrowing power into collateral, reclaim all the outstanding stock and make a bundle? Not really. The catch is that to afford an LBO most companies have to issue junk bonds to cover the debt created by the stock buyback. This means that the company takes on a staggering load of new debt, and at high interest rates, which makes financial health very difficult to achieve and maintain. A business downturn or a bad year or two can prove disastrous to a company awash in junk-bond debt.

Are Junk Bonds a Recent Invention?

Just over ten years ago, a very smart investment banker, Michael Milken of Drexel Burnham, took advantage of a system that had existed since 1909. That system, the Standard & Poor's rating of bonds, grades each bond issued by a company or a municipality as AAA through BB. Any bond with a lesser rating is thought to be unworthy of investment grade rating, hence a "junk bond."

Mr. Milken reasoned, correctly, as it turned out, that investors would be willing to buy such bonds if they were sold cheaply enough, had a high yield and had a reasonable chance of not defaulting. Falling somewhere between investment-grade bonds (very secure) and stocks (always risky), junk bonds give investors a unique market opportunity.

Junk bonds aren't for every investor. People who buy bonds to provide a steady stream of nontaxable income and want those bonds securely backed up (such as municipal bonds) should not take the risks posed by junk bonds. For those with extra cash and lots of nerve, however, they may be just the thing.

Anatomy of an LBO—
Safeway Stores

As attractive as LBO's may be to financial wizards and company owners, they have profound effects on the day-to-day operations of the companies involved. Draconian measures to sell assets and cut staff to reduce the mountain of debt that LBO's create are often necessary. Here's an example of what an LBO meant to a real business and its very real employees.

It used to be that the 175,000 employees of California-based Safeway Stores felt secure. Wages in the highly unionized chain were good, roughly $10 to $12 per hour, as were benefits and the work environment. In 1971, Safeway was the world's largest grocery chain, according to *Mother Jones* magazine, but had been losing market share steadily since then due to competition from other chains.

Until 1987, Safeway had been managed by the same family since 1926. In 1980 Peter Magowan, the thirty-seven-year-old son of Safeway's founder, was appointed chairman. The junior Magowan was determined to restore Safeway to its preeminent position in the supermarket industry by streamlining operations. He also wanted to keep it as a family-owned business.

In 1985 Safeway's annual dividends were $98 million (a 5 percent return on equity for stockholders), revenues were $20 billion and retained earnings were $231 million. Debt was moderate and there was substantial capital available for expansion.

The combination was irresistible to takeover specialists. Safeway's stock was undervalued, meaning that when its assets were considered for their sale value, rather than as part of an ongoing operation, they were worth much more. Top management was inexperienced but determined to hang on, and there were valuable assets—2,365 stores sitting on top of even more valuable land. One drawback was that Safeway was a union shop, but what better way to break a union than with an LBO? In fact, an LBO is a very effective tool for union-busting, because the new management can close stores, factories or other business entities. Unions have nothing to negotiate about if there are no more stores or factories.

In early 1986 Robert and Herbert Haft, a father-and-son team of Wall Street corporate raiders, recognizing Safeway's potential for a hostile takeover, made a run at the company by buying 3 million shares of Safeway stock, or 4.9 percent, just under the limit required for SEC disclosure. As expected, Safeway's Magowan decided to stand and fight the bid. He hired the top LBO legal guns—Wachtell, Lipton, Rosen & Katz—and got input from financial advisers at Merrill Lynch, Morgan Stanley Guaranty and the Bankers Trust Company.

None of the choices that the experts offered Magowan was great:

• buy back millions of Safeway shares on the market, thereby driving the stock price up

• find a friendly buyer ("white knight")

• hinder the takeover on legal technicalities

• engineer a leveraged buyout by borrowing billions of dollars to buy all the stock and take the company private

By June 1986, the Hafts had continued their Safeway stock-buying spree. Since at that point they owned nearly 6 percent of the stock, they were forced to disclose their identity to the SEC. They were ready to be known. With junk-bond champions Drexel Burnham at their side, the Hafts had the potential to raise $3.5 billion of debt to purchase all of Safeway stock. It was time for Magowan to make a decision about the choices confronting him. He opted for the LBO.

Magowan, recognizing the strength of his adversaries, turned to another heavyweight in the LBO world—Kohlberg Kravis Roberts & Co. KKR, engineers of the Beatrice LBO, the largest ever, were very interested in the proposition, and quickly agreed to outbid the Hafts in a move that would put Safeway in private hands.

The bidding war for Safeway shares between the Hafts and KKR escalated in June and July of 1986. The Hafts's final offer was $64 a share, up from $37 at the beginning of the year. KKR's was $69 a share.

Safeway's fate was in the hands of its board of directors. On July 25, 1986, Safeway's board agreed to the LBO by KKR. The Hafts left with a bit more than hurt feelings—$140 million in a "special option," compensation negotiated as cash and securities for their interest (stock) in the company. A special option is necessary for one set of players to leave the playing field wide open for the winning team of investors.

KKR engineered the second-largest LBO to date, using only $130 million in equity to buy a $3.4 billion company! It received:

- $60 million in fees from Safeway for managing the buyout

- $500,000 annually in consulting fees for as long as the companies remain mutually involved, which at press time was at least five years, or through 1992

- 20 percent of the profit its investors make, potentially $200 million

There were some other big winners:

- Bankers Trust, Morgan Stanley and Drexel Burnham divvied up $51 million in banking fees.

- Drexel received $15 million from the Hafts for financing the junk bonds.

- Merrill Lynch garnered nearly $15 million for advisers' fees.

- Legal and accounting fees amounted to $25 million.

- The printing bill for the mountain of documents created was $2.7 million.

What Happened to Safeway?

The LBO created $4.3 billion of new debt for Safeway, a staggering sum. The obvious solution was to sell off pieces of the business to help retire the debt.

In an LBO, a closed grocery store is worth more than an open one selling real food to real people. In addition to being a valuable piece of real estate, it has inventory and equipment. In this case, a closed Safeway store was worth $2 million, an open store much less. It may seem hard to understand why this is so. Why is a closed store worth more than an open one? Because selling off assets such as inventory, equipment, the building and surrounding property generates cash—a great deal more cash than comes in on a day-to-day basis in an ongoing business. The cash benefits the company on a short-term basis and helps it pay off the debt incurred during the process of transacting an LBO. However, the downside is that once a store is closed, that business, the community presence, is gone forever. Even if something else eventually replaces it, the original entity and its spirit cannot be replaced, not to mention the cessation of ongoing revenues from an income-producing business.

Safeway sold nearly one-half of its 2,400 stores. Thirty-seven thousand people lost their jobs. Others had their wages substantially reduced. More than 1,100 neighborhoods lost supermarkets.

Another big loser was the Internal Revenue Service. When Safeway was last publicly traded in 1985, it payed $28 million in federal income tax. In 1987, despite $300 million in operating profits, Safeway reported a loss of $103 million—the interest payments on the LBO-created debt. With $4.3 billion of debt, Safeway will be posting a hefty deduction for ten to fifteen years.

The current Safeway owners will receive $70 million worth of tax-advantaged treatment. Who will pay the tax liability that they've created by turning 37,000 productively employed people into unemployment and welfare recipients? We, the taxpayers, will.

When an LBO Turns Sour

About the only justification for the monumental rewards reaped by LBO specialists is the risk that something will go wrong. That's how the world of finance operates. The greater the risk, the greater the reward. Sometimes, though, the risks and problems resulting from an LBO become almost impossible to manage. This is what happened with the Revco LBO.

At first, an LBO for Revco made a lot of sense as a way for the Ohio-based chain of drugstores to sell off acquisitions not central to the core business of drugstores and to raise needed capital. Revco went private in a 1986 LBO. The $1.3 billion deal was put together by Salomon Brothers, the New York Life Insurance Company and Transcontinental Services Group.

After the buyout everyone seemed to be rolling in money. All of it, however, was debt. Then things started to go wrong. Sales forecasts in the drugstore chain were off by roughly $1 billion, and since earnings declined after the buyout there wasn't enough cash in the till to make an interest payment of $46 million due in June 1988. Assets such as Odd Lot Trading Co. and the Stanton Corporation employment agencies were supposed to be sold to help retire the debt but weren't because there were no buyers ready and willing to make an acceptable offer for these parts of the package. Such critical strategic blunders eventually led to Revco's 1988 bankruptcy filing.

Does America Win?

Government statistics show that from 1983 to 1988, more than $700 billion went into takeovers, mergers and acquisitions, of which LBO's were a significant part. These efforts produced no new plants, no new jobs and no new products. The only two things LBO's create are a handful of multimillionaires and a mountain of debt. Add to that the eventual resale of privately held shares to the public as a way to reduce the debt, and the picture is clear. The Wall Street crowd might be winning, but the American economy, the laid-off employees, the IRS and the original shareholders are losing.

Lest we be presenting an overly passionate critique of the LBO phenomenon, there are some financial experts who see positive results. Conservative economists say that, if stock market values are the measure of success, LBO's make companies stronger because companies "in play" (to be acquired) shoot up in value. Buyout-fund managers and investors in junk bonds can also do very well financially. KKR considers the Safeway buyout a huge success because the company is ahead of schedule in selling assets and on target for cutting debts. Also, Safeway has taken some of the cash generated in the LBO and upgraded its stores so that it can compete with more upscale and lucrative supermarket chains such as Grand Union.

There's also some possible merit to the argument that a privately owned company is run by a management that cares more about what happens than does the more impersonal management and results of a publicly owned company. It's still too early in the "LBO era" to comprehend and assess fully its long-term effects.

The laissez-faire capitalism of the Reagan era unleashed this wave of LBO's, takeovers, mergers and acquisitions whose effects are just now being assessed. Of course, the brilliance and business acumen of people like Michael Milken, the Hafts and those at KKR played an important part in sparking LBO mania. However, in a more tightly regulated business environment, LBO's would be severely curtailed or even prohibited. Perhaps the ever-present threat of more government regulation from the Democratic-controlled Congress actually fanned the flames of the LBO movement. The "let's do it now because tomorrow the party may be over" mentality probably kept deals rolling along.

Whether or not the creation of huge, practically unspendable fortunes for a handful of investors, the ocean of red ink for companies and the reduction of assets and personnel is ultimately good for the American economy remains to be seen.

The SEC is currently striking at the heart of LBO's with an ongoing investigation of those junk-bond junkies at Drexel Burnham, looking for improprieties of "insider trading." Drexel Burnham admitted to certain improprieties and agreed to pay penalties totaling $300 million, half of it to reimburse its customers who may have been hurt in the scam. Drexel also fired its superstar, Michael Milken, and denied him his 1988 bonus of around $200 million. His brother, Lowell, lost half of his bonus and was placed on an unpaid leave of absence. At press time the Milkens are under federal indictment and are awaiting trial.

Legislators are grappling with the issue of who should be the beneficiary of the LBO, with the idea that the original shareholders rather than top management should get the gain, since they, not top management, ultimately own the assets of the company. Congress, understandably nervous about the immense loss of revenue that results from LBO's, and basically uncomfortable with the notion of "insiders" (management) trading on information about the company's financial and operational status unknowable to "outsiders," seems inclined to outlaw LBO's in the near future. The LBO era may be drawing to a close, but it has left its mark irrevocably on the American economy.

Chapter 10

MERGER MANIA

Anyone who received an MBA before the current merger mania struck America had certain notions about capital. When we thought about capital budgeting we described actions that related to the planning and financing of capital outlays, such as for the purchase of new equipment or for the modernization of plant facilities. Such capital-budgeting decisions were a key factor in the long-run profitability of a company, particularly one with only limited investment funds available.

The skill of managers in choosing how to use those funds was based on investing in the company's future, of making a commitment to the further growth of the company. Our capital-budgeting decisions, pre-LBO, seem positively mundane: How do we reduce costs? Expand physical plants? Select equipment in line with long-term goals? Lease or buy a new factory?

Thanks to the folks at Drexel Burnham, KKR and the other corporate raiders, corporate debt has become more important than building factories. Whoever had the bright idea first that most companies' assets were undervalued and that the top managers would do better by making huge personal profits than by building did a great disservice to this country. Many observers of trends in corporate America feel that LBO's and mergers and acquisitions are just the latest and best device of free-wheeling laissez-faire capitalism, and that the huge personal fortunes that accrue to the lucky major and minor shareholders help pump up the economy in a cascade of cash. In fact, a consensus appears to be taking hold among industry experts that takeovers are causing corporate debts to soar and imposing big risks on the new debt-ridden companies. They say that what's most alarming about the phenomenon is the suddenness with which the wave of takeovers has struck, and the irreversibility of dismantling a company. What may seem irresistible in the short term may turn out to be destructive to the economy in the long run.

It used to be that companies made capital-budgeting decisions based on a conservative strategy of improving or replacing equipment, providing a decent rate of return on investment and minimizing income-tax liability. Merger mania has replaced all that with the crushing load of debt, the more debt the better, since debt is tax-deductible. The new game involves assessing asset values correctly so that companies or pieces of the company can be sold.

What do the vultures do after they've valued the assets? They sell them, of course, hoping that they'll somehow be able to fix what's left of the company. Fixing the company doesn't mean restructuring it so that it runs efficiently and profitably. Fixing it means fixing the financing, changing the marketing or changing the management. There's not much attention to building a company here.

Since the business world is not a scientific laboratory, it's hard to come by data that indicate who's right about what merger mania is doing to American industry. Most acquired companies have seen a 10 to 15 percent loss of personnel, but it's hard to say if this has been beneficial. The main question, then, is this: Should the capital generated in a takeover go into the pockets of the top executives, or is it better off being invested in new productive capacity?

A Classic Case

Before the recent spate of mergers and acquisitions got started, one case stands out as a prime example of what can happen when merger mania strikes. It involved four major companies:

- Bendix, a Fortune 500 company manufacturing appliances and other equipment

- Allied Corporation, a maker of electrical equipment

- Martin Marietta, the aerospace contractor

- United Technologies, an aircraft manufacturer

On the raider side there were also many countries heard from:

- Felix Rohatyn (Lazard Freres & Co.)

- Jay Higgins (Salomon Brothers)

- Bruce Wasserstein and Jay Perella (formerly of First Boston, but now in their own investment-banking company)

- Martin Siegel (formerly of Kidder Peabody & Company, Siegel was convicted of SEC violations)

By the time it got all sorted out it was hard to tell the winners from the losers.

It all started in late 1981, when William Agee, president of Bendix, found himself sitting on close to $2 billion in cash (from several years of booming revenues) and searching for a possible takeover candidate that would enhance Bendix's reputation as a high-tech company. After reviewing the field he set out to buy Martin Marietta, headed by Thomas Pownall.

In April 1982 Agee started to buy up MM stock, which was selling cheaply. By August, Bendix announced a tender offer of $43 per share of Martin Marietta stock. Following the tender offer, Agee planned a stock swap for the remainder of MM's approximately 35.8 million outstanding shares. By this maneuver, MM stock would be exchanged for Bendix stock in a still unspecified and negotiable part of the deal.

But Pownall, MM's chief, had different ideas. He didn't

want to be forced out. On news of the takeover attempt, MM stock rose $3 per share. At a hastily called board meeting, Pownall and his board rejected Bendix's offer and announced their own tender offer for Bendix! Pownall's two-part tender offer went like this: 11.9 million of Bendix's 23.7 million shares (more than 50 percent) at $75 per share; a stock swap by MM that would give Bendix shareholders $55 for each of the shares. The average share price of $65 would give the whole transaction a value of $1.5 billion. Pownall's counterstrategy has been called the "Pac Man"™ defense—"let's gobble them up before they swallow us."

Agee, intent on acquiring MM, rejected the deal, and the battle heated up. In came white knight Harry Gray of United Technologies, moving to Martin Marietta's rescue. Pownall and Gray arranged to split Bendix shares between them. Agee quickly arranged golden parachutes—extremely handsome and lucrative retirement settlements—for himself and fifteen other Bendix execs to cushion themselves should they lose .

Bendix and MM were fighting to a standoff. Neither could gain financial control of the other without outside help. By late September 1982, Bendix had spent 12 billion leveraged dollars to buy 70 percent of MM. MM had spent $900 million to buy 50 percent of Bendix and Allied. Allied had spent $1.8 billion to buy all of Bendix and 39 percent of MM. United Technologies didn't buy anything but was waiting in the wings to help out Pownall.

With Bendix, MM and Allied engaged in a borrowing frenzy, the only really happy people were the various advisers—First Boston, Salomon, Kidder Peabody and Lazard Fréres. The top executives of Bendix and Martin Marietta were happy—they had their golden parachutes packed and ready to go.

The Allied Corporation triumphed simply by being the highest bidder, paying an average of $80.00 per share of Bendix stock that had never sold above $67.50 before September 1982. Later, Allied merged with Signal and is now called Allied-Signal, Inc. Allied-Signal then spun off thirty-five of its nonstrategic businesses to Henley Group, Inc., for $300 million and 19.5 million shares of Henley preferred stock.

What Does It All Mean?

Let's step back and gain a little perspective on this whole situation. Many years ago, M&A work (merger and acquisition) used to be a small part of investment banking. Back then the decision to buy or sell Company or Subsidiary X was one aspect of the relationship between banker and client in their overall strategy of building a viable business. The potential acquisition was evaluated as to how it fit into the company's future.

Now the M&A business exists independently, with one magic goal—to make money, lots of it. This represents a dramatic change in the mindset of bankers, who were once thought of as wise and conservative handlers of other people's money. Somehow a certain segment of the investment-banking community decided to shed the traditional practices and values of bankers in favor of a more lively, lucrative and risky approach. The bankers aren't there to give counsel but to pursue, openly and aggressively, high fees for themselves. Building companies or what's good economically in the long run is irrelevant; the means have become the end.

Raiders, the M&A chieftains, are immune to the consequences of what they do. They can close a business forever, lay people off, sell precious assets and make huge fees virtually unchecked. Making matters worse, most M&A deals occur under severe time pressure. Offers, counteroffers and strategies are hatched by people working long hours, sometimes even around the clock. There's rarely time to think the whole thing through, much less an attempt to do so.

What does this mean in real terms for a company like Bendix? Detroit-based Bendix, along with Burroughs and the Big Three automakers, were the only major employers in that area. By closing Bendix, the raiders removed a major employer forever, causing unemployment and depressed real estate values because of the large numbers of people selling their homes. This in turn had an impact on schools, hotels, restaurants and even United Way contributions. Scientific talent and the corporate culture disappeared, gone forever.

Is M&A activity as it currently exists an unacceptable conflict of interest? Investment bankers are out to generate fees, not to build businesses. Top executives get a once-in-a-lifetime opportunity to enhance their personal wealth. Bendix chief Agee guaranteed himself a golden parachute of $9 million in stock options and salary that would be paid to him years after he left the company. Other top executives got similar packages, so why should they care what happens to Bendix?

The End?

In the basic scenario of mergers and acquisitions and leveraged buyouts, the main goal is to make a business profitable within an average of three years. Companies facing short-term difficulties, marginal profits or even losses while building (or rebuilding) a business don't have a chance. This is in contrast to Japan and Europe, where there's a tendency to carry businesses toward a long-range goal.

In the investment-banking world, companies are advised to throw in the towel and give business away to competitors because there's not enough profit. Assets, such as subsidiaries that were acquired because they fit in with overall strategy or buildings that may be valuable pieces of real estate, are sold off. Proceeds go to huge M&A deals, golden parachutes and the like, or to purchase other assets.

A vicious cycle is set in motion—the more business lost and the more corporate overhead, the more each unit costs to produce. Marginal businesses are shed and jobs are lost to foreign competitors. We have to ask: Are stockholders the only constituency, and the stock price a company's only measure of success? Society and government have come to accept M&A work and LBO's as the way things have to be, but perhaps this movement will pass.

Chapter 11

I t hasn't been easy for anyone to move from the simple and knowable financial world of the 1950s and 1960s to the complexities of the early 1990s, where specialists reign.

It feels as if we're on a rapidly accelerating course. As our capacity to process transactions increases, the numbers and kinds of transactions increase, spawning more financial instruments in an ever more sophisticated financial community, a global community. The cycle feeds on itself—the more innovation, the faster the transaction processing, the more involvement from different economies that want to participate. We haven't slowed down long enough to begin contemplating the long range results of all this activity.

In the midst of all this economic expansion there is a counterbalancing force: the trend to be "lean and mean," to cut excess staff and productive capacity. This all means there is the emergence of a more focused, specialized business community in which companies and individuals have to take on more work than ever before, work that has to be done right.

If the world is moving so fast, how can you, an individual investor or person contemplating a financial career, hope to make sense out of this complexity? Can you do anything but react and try to hang on to the tiger's tail? The answer is a qualified "yes." Success will come by specialization, honing in on what is of interest to you and following trends in that area. This reflects the trend toward specialization in the business community.

Let's review for a moment our basic tools. By now you should have a very good idea of what interests you in the world—financially, that is—and some idea of how to get it. Perhaps you've selected some types of investments that appeal to you, investments that you want to track over time. With practice, you should become increasingly adept at an intelligent reading every day of both *The New York Times* and *The Wall Street Journal*. If you're more adventurous, you may even try using your personal computer both to follow financial news and to check out promising investments. Hopefully, you've even written a basic financial plan outlining your objectives and the steps you'll take to get there. What's next?

At the same time that you've been focusing and narrowing your interests, financial institutions have been doing the same, which will make your life a whole lot easier. Certainly, there have been mergers and acquisitions and the formation of mega-giant financial companies that have emerged as global competitors. But within those firms various divisions and subsidiaries exist to service their particular market niches. They look to optimize results by developing market segments that spring from particular strengths. They pay close attention to controlling costs, to risk management and to credit analysis. The Japanese are already masters of this market segmentation approach. They isolate growing market segments, hone them with precision and watch them perform at maximum efficiency.

Unfortunately, the days of personal service are fading fast, to be replaced by super-efficient information processors who are supposed to do the job quickly and without fuss or muss. Don't lose heart, though. We may see the return of some personal service in the financial sector in the 1990s. Remember, the strong growth sector is for companies with market niches, not the mass market. Government statistics show that small companies are enjoying a resurgence in the United States. Companies with fewer than 500 workers added 1.2 million jobs in America between 1976 and 1984, while large manufacturers lost over 300,000 jobs. Companies with 250 employees or less could comprise 50 percent of total employers by the mid-1990s, up from 42 percent today.

Knowing what we now know about the direction in which the financial community is headed is very important. However, knowing about something won't necessarily help you capitalize on it. Knowing won't make you rich unless you do something to act on that knowledge, just as we learned with our steps to financial planning. The key is to take action based on information.

Taking action may be divided into concrete steps:

Step 1. Go back to your objectives from your financial plan. Review them and ask questions like these:

• Based on the trends I'm reading about, should I change my investment strategy?

• If the trend is toward smaller companies, is now a good time for me join a smaller company? Or to go out on my own?

• I think my company is a likely target for an LBO. Can I afford to plan for early retirement?

Step 2. Based on your questions and answers, you will come up with a plan.

Step 3. With your plan in mind, you need to learn to update your thinking and forecast appropriately.

Step 4. Strategy implementation. Based on what you know and your constantly updated forecasts, it's simply a matter of doing what you have to do, whether it's changing your investment strategy or changing your job, to accomplish your goals.

GLOSSARY

arbitrage: the simultaneous purchase and sale of the same securities, commodities or foreign currency in different markets to profit from unequal prices

assets: things that are owned and have monetary value

ATM: automated teller machine

balance sheet: called the "statement of financial position," it breaks down the company's finances into assets, liabilities and capital

blue chip: a company generally acknowledged for the quality of its products or services

bond: promissory note by which the issuer gives evidence of debt and promises to pay the bearer a specified amount of interest for a certain period of time

capital: the interest, most often financial, of the owners in an enterprise

cash flow: revenues less expenses

CATS: Certificates of Accrual on Treasury Securities

CBOE: Chicago Board of Options Exchange, which promotes the trading of options

CD: a certificate of deposit; a fixed-rate savings certificate with a set maturity date

computer-aided investing: using electronic bulletin board services and public utilities to help make investment decisions

coupon bond: a bond with interest coupons attached; the coupons are clipped as they come due and are surrendered for payment

depreciation: charges against earnings to write off the cost, less salvage value, of an asset over its useful estimated life

DJI: the Dow Jones Industrials average; thirty blue-chip stocks whose changes are calculated and expressed as moving up or down, relative to the previous market's close

equity: the excess of value in an asset over the debt balance

FDIC: the Federal Deposit Insurance Corporation, the governmental regulatory agency that insures deposits in commercial banks

GAAP: Generally Accepted Accounting Principles; a standard set of rules developed by the accounting profession for the preparation of financial statements

hedging: linking two or more securities into one investment position to reduce risk

investment banker: the middleperson between the corporation issuing new securities and the public; the investment banker forms a syndicate to sell or distribute large blocks of stock

IRA: Individual Retirement Account; for deferred retirement income, supplemental to a corporate pension plan

junk bond: a non-rated bond issued by a company to manage the debt created by a leveraged buyout

Keogh: a retirement program for the self-employed and their employees based on tax-deferred savings

LBO: leveraged buyout; a deal whereby a publicly owned company is taken private by using the company's assets as collateral

LDC: less-developed countries economically—*e.g.,* the Philippines, Kenya

leverage: using the equity in one asset to acquire another asset

liabilities: amounts owed to outsiders

liquidity: the ability to buy or sell a security or other asset in a short period of time at or near its market value

LYONs: Liquid-Yield-Option Zero Notes

merchant banking: the middle market, mostly asset-backed, lending to medium-size businesses with revenues of between $5 million and $50 million

MUFF: Multi-Option Funding Facilities

munis: municipal securities; debt obligations of states, their political subdivisions and certain agencies

NASDAQ: National Association of Security Dealers of Automated Quotations, an index reflecting OTC (over the counter) market activity based on an automated information network

net worth: amount of equity in assets owned

NIC: newly industrialized countries—*e.g.,* Hong Kong and Singapore

OECD: Organization for Economic Cooperation and Development; members are fully industrialized nations—*e.g.,* U.S. and Japan

option: the right to buy (call) or sell (put) a fixed amount of a stock at a specified price within a limited period of time

P/E ratio: price-to-earnings ratio; the current market price of a stock divided by the previous year's per share earnings

primary financial centers: New York, London, Tokyo—where the world's major stock exchanges are located

raider: an investment banker who earns high fees for arranging acquisitions and LBO's

retail broker: a full-service, full-price stock brokerage house

RICO: Racketeer-Influenced and Corrupt Organizations Act; a governmental vehicle for prosecution of trading violations

RUF: Revolving Underwriting Facilities

SEC: the Securities Exchange Commission, established by Congress to protect investors against irregularities in the trading of financial instruments

secondary financial center: Hong Kong, Singapore, Frankfurt and Paris

secondary market: a market such as NYSE or OTC where previously issued securities may be bought or sold

securitization: using a current asset as collateral to acquire another asset

S&P: the Standard and Poor's average; like the DJI, this average compares the activity of industrials, transporation and utility stocks from the previous day's closings

STAG: Sterling Transferable Accruing Government security

tax-deferred income: cash flow on which no tax is legally payable

tender offer: an offer made by one corporation to purchase the stock of another corporation at a specific price and a specific time

T-bills: treasury bills, U.S. government issues having an original maturity of less than one year

TIGR: Treasury Income Growth Receipts

TRUF: Transferable Revolving Underwriting Facilities

unbundled stock unit: a mechanism whereby each share of preferred stock is divided into three separate securities to increase the stockholder's value per share

unit investment trust: a tax-exempt portfolio of municipal bonds with a minimum investment of $1,000

user-friendly: a computer program designed to be simple to use for non-experts

whole-life insurance: any life insurance other than term that has a cash value that can be borrowed, used as collateral or withdrawn by surrendering the policy

ZEBRA: Zero-coupon Eurosterling Bearer of Registered Securities

SUGGESTED READING

BOOKS

The Complete Guide to Personal Investing
Gary Klott, Times Books, New York, NY, 1987

Economics in Perspective
John Kenneth Galbraith, Houghton-Mifflin, New York, NY, 1987

The 15-Minute Investor
Chet Currier & The Associated Press, The Associated Press, New York, NY, 1986

The Handbook for No-Load Fund Investors
Sheldon Jacobs, Dow-Jones Irwin, New York, NY, 1988

Making Money
Howard Ruff, Simon & Schuster, New York, NY,1984

The Money Book of Money
Robert Klein, Little Brown & Co., Boston, MA, 1987

The Predator's Ball
Connie Bruck, Simon & Schuster, New York, NY, 1988

Smart Investing: A Step By Step Guide
Andrew Senchak, Taylor Publishing, Dallas, Texas, 1987

INDEX

ABOUT THE AUTHOR

Marlene C. Piturro, Ph.D., is a businesswoman, author, educator and psychologist who has served as an internal/ external consultant to organizations in the private and public sectors. She received her Ph.D. in clinical psychology from Fordham University, and her M.B.A. in management information systems/finance from Iona College.

Dr. Piturro worked as an internal consultant to a major commercial bank on the global banking unit before devoting her efforts to teaching, writing and consulting. She teaches at the Business School at Cornell University's New York State Institute of Industrial and Labor Relations and at the State University of New York at Empire. She has written for a number of national publications, including *Working Woman, Reader's Digest, Management Review* and the *Journal of Commerce.* Her monthly column dealing with career development strategies, "Reorient for Reentry," has appeared in a regional newspaper for three years.

If you're mystified by the buzz-word world of business insiders and MBAs, then **BUSINESS SMARTS**—offering straightforward, accessible, entertaining advice about the basics of business—is for you! Look for these handy guides from **Price Stern Sloan:**

ACCOUNTING MADE EASY

A critical aspect of any business, accounting is also one of the most intimidating. *Accounting Made Easy* shows how to decipher annual reports and balance sheets, explains how the accounting profession works and details the changing face of the industry today.

ADVERTISING MADE EASY

This is an inside look at a fast, frenzied, and extremely attractive field—the arduous winning and maintaining of accounts, creating and selling effective product campaigns, developing and forecasting budgets, assessing media opportunities and more.

MARKETING MADE EASY

Any product must have great marketing to be successful. *Marketing Made Easy* covers all the essentials: product placement and promotion, product life-cycle and positioning, how product and profit are tied to price variations and more.